PSYCHOLOGY RESEARCH PROGRESS

ANTISOCIAL BEHAVIOR

PERSPECTIVES, MANAGEMENT STRATEGIES AND OUTCOMES

Psychology Research Progress

Additional books in this series can be found on Nova's website under the Series tab.

Additional e-books in this series can be found on Nova's website under the eBooks tab.

PSYCHOLOGY RESEARCH PROGRESS

ANTISOCIAL BEHAVIOR

PERSPECTIVES, MANAGEMENT STRATEGIES AND OUTCOMES

ABBY DOBSON
AND
PETER TALBOT
EDITORS

nova
science publishers
New York

Library of Congress Cataloging-in-Publication Data

ISBN: 978-1-53612-954-0

Published by Nova Science Publishers, Inc. † New York

CONTENTS

PREFACE

In this compilation, the authors offer supplementary support to the idea that temperament theory is essential to developing upon the understanding of the etiology of antisocial behavior (and criminal justice) by documenting a basis for why the sex of the child is the strongest predictor of antisocial behavior. Additionally, a study is presented on the relationship between residents' ASB perceptions and their levels of participation in housing management in private multi-owned housing developments. The authors developed an analytic model exemplifying how ASB perceptions can have a catalytic effect on resident participation in multi-owned housing developments management. The model was tested based on the findings of a structured questionnaire survey on residents of private multi-owned housing developments in Hong Kong. A chapter is included wherein the definition of dating violence and the different types of gender violence are expressed, as well as the mechanisms operating in situations of intimate partner violence during adolescence. The predominant causes of violence, grounded in the Ecological Systems Theory of Human Development, are outlined. The book ends by deliberating on some of the core behavioral problems in adolescence in the school environment, especially bullying. The authors analyze the characteristics of aggressors and victims involved in these situations, as well as the role of bystanders, and an outline of intervention strategies is provided.

Chapter 1 - Although temperamental traits have long been understood to be important constructs for understanding normal and abnormal development, their relevance to criminal justice has only recently been recognized. This paper extended this belated recognition to an examination of how sex differences in temperamental traits contribute to the massive sex difference in the severest forms of antisocial behavior by conducting a qualitative/narrative review of the literature relevant to sex differences in temperamental traits was conducted. A sex difference in at least three broad temperamental dimensions was identified. The dimensions involve attention/regulation processes, activity level, and emotionality. A sex difference on these dimensions results in males being more likely to be behaviorally and emotionally impulsive, being more easily socialized into physical aggression, and being less fearful and empathic and therefore less likely to internalize rules. A plausible biological mechanism mediating each of these sex differences was also provided.

Chapter 2 - The problem of antisocial behavior (ASB) or minor incivilities in housing has attracted extensive public attention in many jurisdictions. In spite of the deployment of various approaches, ranging from family intervention and probationary tenancies to statutory orders, the ASB problem still proliferates in most places. As suggested in the literature, ASB can result in reduced residential satisfaction, poor physical and mental health and social disruption. However, how ASB affects the decision or behavior of residents in housing management participation has been ignored in previous studies. Hypothetically, the impacts of ASB can influence resident participation in both directions. On one hand, residents tend to participate more actively in housing management when they cannot tolerate the ASB in their living places and want to make a change. On the other hand, proliferation of ASB problem may weaken the social tie and bonding within a residential neighborhood, leading to the dwindled willingness of the residents to participate in collective actions in housing management. This study aims to explore the link between residents' ASB perceptions and their levels of participation in housing management in private multi-owned housing (MOH) developments empirically. An analytic model illustrating how ASB perceptions can have a catalytic effect on resident participation in MOH management is developed. Based on the findings of a structured questionnaire survey on residents of private MOH in Hong Kong, the model was tested using a path-analytic technique. The analysis results show that ASB perceptions affect private housing residents' participation levels in MOH management. Policy recommendations then follow.

Chapter 3 - This short communication focuses on violent behavior perpetrated in adolescents' first romantic relationships, a fact that can establish behavioral patterns for future relations in adulthood. The first section of this chapter includes the definition of dating violence and the different types of gender violence, as well as the mechanisms operating in situations of intimate partner violence during adolescence. Following this, the main causes of violence, grounded in the Ecological Systems Theory of Human Development, are outlined. Finally, the consequences of such behavior for victims are analyzed. The chapter ends with a summary of the main ideas and provides some final recommendations for prevention.

Chapter 4 - In the school context, some children and adolescents show particular behavioral problems which are inappropriate for their age and have negative consequences for others or themselves. In this regard, one of the problems that currently generates more concern in society is antisocial behavior in educational settings, and especially situations known as bullying. These acts, mostly committed by adolescents, have an increasing prevalence and serious consequences for victims and aggressors, and contaminate the general social environment at school. This short communication addresses these topics, defines some of the main behavioral problems in adolescence in the school environment, including bullying, as well as the main characteristics of aggressors and victims involved in such situations, and the role of bystanders. In addition, an outline is given of some intervention strategies for treating and preventing the different problems of behavior at school.

In: Antisocial Behavior ISBN: 978-1-53612-954-0
Editors: Abby Dobson and Peter Talbot © 2017 Nova Science Publishers, Inc.

Chapter 1

THE DIFFERENCE IN SEX CONCERNING THE PREVALENCE OF SEVERE ANTISOCIAL BEHAVIORS: A TEMPERAMENT-BASED EXPLANATION

Robert Eme**, PhD
Illinois School of Professional Psychology at Argosy University, Schaumburg Campus, Chicago, Illinois, US

ABSTRACT

Although temperamental traits have long been understood to be important constructs for understanding normal and abnormal development, their relevance to criminal justice has only recently been recognized. This paper extended this belated recognition to an examination of how sex differences in temperamental traits contribute to the massive sex difference in the severest forms of antisocial behavior by conducting a qualitative/narrative review of the literature relevant to sex differences in temperamental traits was conducted. A sex difference in at least three broad temperamental dimensions was identified. The dimensions involve attention/regulation processes, activity level, and emotionality. A sex difference on these dimensions results in males being more likely to be behaviorally and emotionally impulsive, being more easily socialized into physical aggression, and being less fearful and

* Corresponding Author Email: reme@argosy.edu.

empathic and therefore less likely to internalize rules. A plausible biological mechanism mediating each of these sex differences was also provided.

INTRODUCTION

Sex differences are often associated with large phenotypic variation within species (Parsch & Ellegren, 2013). It is therefore not surprising that sex is widely acknowledged as an important factor in understanding individual differences in many behaviors (Stewart & McDermott, 2004). Indeed, as Thomas Insel, former director of the National Institute of Mental Health observed, "It's pretty difficult to find any single factor that's more predictive for some of these disorders than gender" (Holden, 2005, p. 1574). The validity of Insel's observation has no better illustration than the sex difference in the prevalence of three of the most severe antisocial behaviors defined as behaviors that violate social and legal norms (Eisner & Malti, 2015). These behaviors are chronic physical aggression, violence, and life-course–persistent antisocial behavior. Indeed, males so far exceed females in the prevalence of these behaviors that can be characterized as being almost exclusively male (Eme, 2014). Thus, Tremblay (2010) has aptly observed that of all the risk factors for the development of antisocial behavior, sex of the child is by far the most robust predictor.

Recently DeLisi and Vaughn (2014) have made a persuasive case for a temperament-based theory of antisocial behavior. They noted that despite the fact that there have been thousands of published works in multiple disciplines on various temperamental constructs, these constructs, which are "essential to criminal justice, are relatively new to it (p. 19)." This paper will extend the work of DeLisi and Vaughn (2014) on temperament to an examination of how sex differences in temperament contribute to the massive sex difference in antisocial behavior.[1] The paper will begin with a discussion of some general concepts of temperament. It will then examine in detail how sex differences in specific temperamental traits increase risk for antisocial behavior. It will conclude with a discussion of how the interplay of temperament with environment and temperament x temperament interactions can magnify the effect of even small sex differences in temperament.

[1] For a discussion of environmental/social learning factors that help explain the sex difference, the interested reader can consult Russell, Robins, and Odgers (2014).

TEMPERAMENT

It has long been known that from early infancy onward children differ from one another in early developing, biologically rooted behavioral and emotional reactions to the environment (Kagan, 2013; Krieger & Stringaris, 2016; Rothbart, 2012). Such individual differences, which have come to be known as temperament, are influenced across development by genes, maturation, experience, and gene x environment interactions. It is commonly accepted that temperament influences the development of personality, although clarification is needed to identify the precise processes whereby this takes place (Chen & Schmidt, 2015; Stifter & Dollar, 2016).

Beginning with the with ancient belief linking the four humors (blood, yellow bile, black bile, phlegm) to the different temperaments of sanguine, choleric, melancholic, and phlegmatic types, there has been a long tradition linking temperament to the development of various forms of psychopathology, including antisocial behavior (Stifter & Dollar, 2016). Perhaps the most useful way to conceptualize this linkage is to view temperament as a component in what becomes a dynamic process of transactions between the child and the environment, gradually producing different adjustment outcomes (Bates, Schermerhorn, & Petersen, 2014). At least seven different models have been proposed to explain how these complex transactions can result in the development of various disorders (Stifter & Dollar, 2016). Among these various models, the vulnerability model incorporates many of the proposed links between temperament and psychopathology that have been posited by the other models (Martel, Gremillion, & Tackett, 2014; Stifter & Dollar, 2016). This model, which is analogous to the classic, widely accepted diathesis-stress model of psychopathology (Stifter & Dollar, 2016), proposes that extreme levels of temperamental dimensions[2] place an individual at increased risk for developing various disorders because they render the individual more vulnerable to the pathogenic elements of whatever environments they are exposed to. In addition, additive effects are possible such that multiple

[2] Terms such as "dimensions," dispositions," and "tendencies" have been used to describe how temperament affects individual differences in behavior, with "trait" being used most frequently when discussing personality (Rothbart, 2012). These various terms reflect the historically vexing issue of disentangling temperament, which is presumed to develop very earlier in life, from personality, which is presumed to develop more slowly (Nigg, 2006). Several authors have proposed that the term "trait" can be applied to both temperament and personality (Martel, 2013; Rothbart, 2012). Rothbart (2012) views temperamental traits as a subset of personality traits. I use the terms dimension and trait interchangeably when referring to temperament.

temperamental vulnerabilities linearly increase the child's risk for developing antisocial behavior.

Although there is still debate over the precise dimensional structure of temperament (Bates et al., 2014; Chen & Schmidt, 2015; Krieger & Stringaris, 2016), there is a convergence on three broad dimensions (from which subdimensions emerge) which are most relevant to explaining the sex difference in severe antisocial behavior: *Attention/Regulation, Activity Level,* and *Emotionality* (Stifter & Dollar, 2016).

The relation of these dimensions to the development of antisocial behavior and sex differences on these dimensions will now be discussed. Each discussion will have four components. First, the temperamental dimension itself will be discussed. Second, the vulnerability that an extreme level of the dimension confers in increasing the risk for antisocial behavior will be presented. Third, a sex difference on temperamental trait will be documented.[3] Lastly, a plausible proximate biological factor[4] explaining the sex difference on the dimension will be presented. This last component is especially appropriate given the "explosion of published biosocial criminological research" during the past ten years (Beaver & Connolly, 2015, p.46), as well as the National Institute of Mental Health's strategic plan for research on mental disorders emphasizing the investigation of the biological basis of mental disorders (National Institute of Mental Health, 2015) and their linkage with the range of environmental factors that influence such disorders.

ATTENTION/REGULATION

Regulation is the "process that modulates (e.g., increases, decreases, or maintains emotional and behavioral reactivity, and attention is foundational to this ability" (Stifter & Dollar, 2016, p. 555). Because of the importance of *self-control* or *self-regulation*, which are equivalent terms for most author for a

[3] Although the vulnerability model emphasizes a sex difference in *extreme* levels of a temperamental trait, less extreme manifestations of the trait can also increase risk if there is a sex difference in the variability of the trait. Namely, even when a mean difference between the sexes is small, there may be a large sex difference in the tails, or extreme ends of the distribution (Halpern, 2012).

[4] *Proximate* explanations focus on present processes/causes of how a behavior or organism functions. *Ultimate* explanations focus on the past evolutionary forces that helped shape the proximate processes. For discussions of the evolutionary roots of these proximate biological sex differences in temperament (which are beyond the scope of this paper), the interested reader can consult Campbell (2013; 2016), Da Silva, Rijo, and Salekin (2015), Del Guidice and Ellis (2016), Martel (2013).

diverse number of fields, there is a variety of terminology to describe self-regulation (McClelland, Geldhof, Cameron, & Wanless, 2015).

Effortful control (EC), which is particularly associated with impulsivity and Attention-Deficit/Hyperactivity Disorder (ADHD)[5] (Eisenberg et al., 2013; Krieger & Stringaris, 2016; Martel, 2013; Nigg, 2016; Stifter & Dollar, 2016) was coined by personality scholars to describe the temperamental precursor to the personality trait of conscientiousness (McClelland et al., 2015).

EFFORTFUL CONTROL

EC can be defined as the "ability to inhibit a dominant response in order to perform and subdominant response, to detect errors, and to engage in planning" (Stifter & Dollar, 2016, p. 570). Because control is deliberate and therefore requires effort it was designated EC to distinguish it from more reactive forms of regulation (Stifter & Dollar, 2016). EC also includes the abilities to shift and focus attention when needed, and to inhibit inappropriate behavior or activate behavior when one does not want to do so (Eisenberg et al., 2013). In short, EC is the temperamental disposition to exercise self-regulation when doing so is difficult (Diamond, 2013).

Vulnerability

EC is hypothesized to affect children's developmental trajectories by contributing to their ability to process information and modulate emotions, behaviors and thoughts (Stifter & Dollar, 2016. As reviewed by Stifter and Dollar (2016), a low level of EC is the temperamental vulnerability most often linked to the development of antisocial behavior, even after controlling for other risk factors since by definition impairment in the ability to inhibit inappropriate impulses and follow societal norms is expected to increase the likelihood of antisocial behavior (Tackett, Martel, & Kushner, 2012). Numerous studies have shown that impaired EC is linked to juvenile and adult

[5] Impulsivity, which can be conceptualized as the personality trait that develops from the temperamental dimension of EC. ADHD (hyperactive/impulsive or combined presentations), represents one the most extreme expressions of impulsivity (Zisner & Beauchaine, 2016) and as such ADHD is the paradigmatic disorder of impaired self-control (Nigg, 2016).

criminal behavior (DeLisi & Vaughn, 2014). It has been associated with antisocial behavior in toddlers and preschoolers as well as in later childhood and preadolescence. The relationship between EC and antisocial behavior is stable and changes in EC are related to changes in children's antisocial behavior. Hence it becomes readily apparent why interest in regulation or self-control unites all behavioral and social sciences, and why impaired self-control, which is more important than socioeconomic status or IQ in predicting crime (Poulton, Moffitt, & Silva, 2015), may be the single most important variable in explaining developmental origins of antisocial behavior (Moffitt, 2012; Moffitt et al., 2011).

Sex Difference

A meta-analysis by Else-Quest, Hyde, Goldsmith and Van Hulle (2006) reported a large sex difference in EC disfavoring males ($d = -1.01$), and greater male variability. Subsequent research supports this sex difference (Else-Quest, 2012).

Biological Basis

Research on sex differences in brain organization has found greater overall anatomical and functional connectivity in individual networks in the adult female than in the adult male brain (Ingalhalikar et al., 2013; Tomasi & Volkow, 2012a). These findings have received strong support from the first study to analyze the brain as whole to provide insight into the organization and integration of individual brain networks known as the structural connectome (Ingalhalikar et al., 2013). The study analyzed the structural connectome in a large sample of 949 (ages 8–22 years; 428 males, 521 females). Results revealed fundamental sex differences in structural architecture of the human brain. During development, male brains are structured to optimize intrahemispheric communication, whereas female brains are structured to optimize interhemispheric communication. These findings suggest that women's higher brain connectivity may optimize functions that require integration and synchronization across large cortical networks such as executive attention (Tomasi, personal communication, July 13, 2013), which in turn may contribute to their higher level of EC.

Impulsivity

The trait of impulsivity can be defined as a "preference for immediate rewards over larger delayed rewards and reflected in actions that are socially inappropriate, maladaptive, and enacted without consideration of consequences" (Zisner & Beauchaine, 2016, p. 184).This broad definition should not be interpreted as indicating that impulsivity is a unitary construct, as current research and theory suggests it comprises several different components that underlie various forms of impulsive behavior (Cross, Copping, & Campbell, 2011; Sharma, Markson, & Clark, 2014; Nigg, 2016). One such trait, designated "disinhibition vs. constraint/conscientiousness," reflects impulsive behaviors that arise from lack of planning, or failure to persist in the face of challenges. This is related strongly to antisocial behaviors (Sharma et al., 2014), and closely reflects the Diagnostic and Statistical Manual of Mental Disorders-5 (DSM-5) ADHD symptoms such as "impatience, difficulty in delaying responses, and frequently interrupting and intruding on others" (American Psychiatric Association, 2013, p. 60).

Vulnerability

There is widespread agreement that *DSM*-defined behavioral impulsivity is a major vulnerability to development of more severe antisocial behavior (Beauchaine & McNulty, 2013; Beauchaine, Shader & Hinshaw, 2016; Castellanos-Ryan & Sequin, 2016; Zisner & Beauchaine, 2016). This vulnerability interacts with environmental risk factors to promote progression along an antisocial pathway the externalizing spectrum (Beauchaine & McNulty, 2013; Beauchaine et al., 2016). Children with ADHD and ODD are particularly likely to progress toward and/or engage in delinquent behavior when reared in environments characterized by various psychosocial adversities such as hostile and inconsistent parenting, maltreatment, and neighborhood violence/criminality (Beauchaine et al., 2016). Although only about half of such children become delinquent, since Robins (1966, 1978) classic study it has been known that antisocial adult males "almost always follow a life-course trajectory that begins in preschool with ADHD, followed by ODD in elementary school; deviant peer group affiliations in middle school; development of CD, substance abuse and dependency in high school; antisocial personality development in young adulthood; and incarceration and recidivism" (Beauchaine et al., 2016, p. 489).

Sex Difference

Research on ADHD provides strong support for a sex difference in behavioral impulsivity among children. In epidemiological studies of ADHD—for which referral bias is unlikely—males outnumber females on the hyperactive-impulsive dimension by a ratio of 3:1 (Willcutt, 2012). In addition to the sex difference in the rate of ADHD, males also experience more severe symptoms of ADHD than females (Arnett, Pennington, Willcutt, DeFries, & Olson, 2015).

Biological Basis

There are at least two possible biological bases for the sex difference in trait impulsivity. First, in the dual-pathway model of ADHD, dysfunction is posited in either the frontostriatal (mesolimbic) pathway, which mediates bottom-up processing of incentive salience including reward responding, and/or the ventromedial prefrontal (mesocortical) pathway, which mediates top-down executive control of attention and emotion (Castellanos-Ryan & Seguin, 2016; Nigg, 2016; Zisner & Beauchaine, 2016). Early in life, behavioral impulsivity is mediated by deficiencies in the bottom-up mesolimbic pathway. This dysfunction includes lower tonic mesolimbic dopamine levels and less phasic dopamine responding to rewards (Zisner & Beauchaine, 2016). Those with ADHD engage in excessive-reward seeking behaviors—expressed as hyperactivity-impulsivity—in part to up-regulate this underresponsivity, which is experienced as an aversive mood state (Zisner & Beauchaine, 2016). Importantly, there appear to be large sex differences in mesolimbic dopamine system dysfunction, which is observed consistently among children with the hyperactive-impulsive and combined presentations of ADHD (Campo, Chamberlain, Sahakian, & Robbins, 2011; Martel, 2013; Tomasi & Volkow, 2012b). As reviewed by Martel (2013), healthy adult males appear to have a lower presynaptic dopamine tone and lower extrastriatal dopamine receptor density and availability compared with healthy adult females. A limitation of these findings is that, to my knowledge, similar studies have yet to be conducted with children.

In addition, deficiencies in the top-down mesocortical system primarily involving the prefrontal cortex and the anterior cingulate cortex that causes a breakdown in communication with the midbrain region can also result in impulsivity. This impulsivity is evidenced in impaired *response inhibition* defined as an impaired ability to suppress a pre-potent response (Nigg, 2016) and *affective decision making* defined as an impaired ability to reflect on the consequences of a choice (Castellanos-Ryan & Seguin, 2016; Nigg, 2016). Moreover, males may be more vulnerable to a dysfunction in this system through an interaction of a sex-linked gene such as the low activity variant of the monoamine oxidase A gene (*MAOA-L*) with an environmental variable such as maltreatment. MAOA is a gene on the X chromosome which codes for the enzyme monoamine oxidase A and is expressed throughout the brain (Dorfman & Buckholtz, 2015). This enzyme degrades (i.e., 'mops up') the monamimes, especially serotonin, following reuptake from the synaptic cleft, thereby rendering it inactive (Dorfman & Buckholtz, 2015). The low activity variant of this gene (MAOA-L) is less efficient in degrading serotonin than the high activity variant (MAOA-H) which results in a higher concentration of intracellular serotonin than the high activity variant (Dorfman & Buckholtz, 2015). In a landmark study, Caspi et al., (2002) reported an interaction between MAOA-L and maltreatment which greatly increased risk for antisocial behavior in males. A meta-analysis (Byrd & Manuck, 2014) and a systematic review (Weeland, Overbeek, de Castro, & Matthys, 2015) provides strong confirmation of the Caspi et al., (2002) finding. In addition, although earlier studies were less consistent in finding an interaction with other environmental adversities (Weeland et al., 2015), more recently such interactions have been found for harsh parenting (Choe, Shaw, Hyde, & Forbes, 2014) and exposure to high levels of violence (Ouellet-Morin et al., 2016). Again, in contrast to earlier studies (e.g., Caspi et al., 2002) more recent research has found evidence for a main effect of the gene on violence in male offenders (Stetler et al., 2014, Tiihonen et al., 2015), with the Tiihonen and colleagues study offering the striking suggestion that "at least 5-10% of all severe violent crime in Finland" is attributable to the gene (p. 786).

In conclusion, despite some null results which may be due the environmental adversity not being severe enough to potentiate the vulnerability (Ouellet-Morin et al., 2016), there is robust support from numerous studies (involving mostly males)[6] for MAOA-L, especially in

[6] There has been much less research on females because females in contrast to males can have a heterozygous genotype in which there are two different alleles at the marker locus on the chromosome (i.e., one X carries the MAOA-H gene and the other X carries the MAOA-L gene). This heterozygous genotype which, for example, characterized 46% of the Caspi and colleagues. sample (2002) makes inferences about high or low activity uncertain (Kim-Cohen et al., 2006).

Furthermore, there has been the puzzling finding in some studies that in contrast to male populations, in female populations there was a significant interaction between

interaction with various environment adversities (Goldman & Rosser, 2014), as a genetic vulnerability which increases risk for the development of antisocial behavior. This vulnerability appears to be due to disruptive effects of the higher concentration of serotonin during critical periods of development on corticolimbic circuits for emotional arousal and regulation which early maltreatment exacerbates, thereby increasing risk for impulsive aggression (Byrd & Manuck, 2014; Dorfman & Buckholtz, 2015; Goldman & Rosser, 2014). Because males are approximately three times more likely than females (37% vs. 12%) to have this genotype (Eme, 2013), there is significant support for a sex-specific genetic effect that increases male risk for antisocial behavior.

Activity Level

Activity level refers to tempo and vigor of energetic behavior (Stifter & Dollar, 2016). It is comprised of a number of additional subdimensions, including high-intensity pleasure, as exemplified by *rough and tumble play* (R&T; Else-Quest, 2012), which is synonymous with play fighting (Geary, 2010, 2015; Pellis & Pellis, 2011). R&T, which was used originally to describe play chasing, fleeing, and wrestling among rhesus monkeys (Fry, 2005), is the most common form of play among male mammals and typically involves components such as chasing, wrestling, pouncing and jumping on partners, pushing, etc. (Geary, 2010, 2015).

Vulnerability

Play fighting is blend of competition and cooperation (Pellis & Pellis, 2011). It is competitive in humans, because participants attempt to gain some advantage over one another, such as throwing and pinning the partner to the ground. It is cooperative and thus differs from physical aggression because participants usually do not take advantage of their success in a way that occurs in real fighting. The universal distribution of R&T among mammals and among humans across virtually every culture suggests that it evolved to serve the adaptive functions of allowing practice of fighting skills under safe

environmental adversity and MAOA-H in predicting antisocial behavior (Holz et al., 2016; Weeland et al, 2015). Little is known about how this sex difference might be explained (Weeland et al., 2015).

conditions, and establishment and maintenance of immediate or long term social dominance necessary for success in one-on-one competitions, one manifestation of which is physical aggression (Archer, 2009; Buss, 2012; Geary, 2010, 2015; Martel, 2013; Pinker, 2011). From an evolutionary perspective, success in dominance aggression served as a solution to several adaptive problems, including enhancing reproductive success (Buss, 2012).

However, despite the cooperative component, play fighting can become a vulnerability because it frequently puts males "on the verge of aggression" (Maccoby, 1998, p. 51). In fact, teachers often have difficulty telling the difference between play fighting and real fighting, and see play fighting as problematic because it can turn into real fighting (Blackmore, Berenbaum, & Liben, 2008). Play fighting increases in frequency during the juvenile years and then declines slowly, often merging into real fighting during adolescence (Geary, 2010).

Sex Difference

Research on activity level has consistently found that boys are more active and impulsive, and more likely to derive pleasure from engaging in high-intensity activities than girls (Else-Quest et al., 2006, 2012). Furthermore, the sex difference in R&T is much larger than for high-intensity-pleasure (Geary, 2010, 2015). By the time they are 3 years old, boys in all societies in which it has been studied begin to enthusiastically engage in R&T, or play fighting (Geary, 2010, 2015). Although girls do engage in R&T, males do so much more frequently and with more vigor and greater zest. This sex difference is most evident with groups of three or more children when adults are not present. Absent adult supervision, groups of boys engage in R&T three to six times more frequently than girls. The difference peaks between ages 8 and 10, and increases in roughness as boys enter puberty, where the distinction between play and genuine physical aggression begins to dissolve. Furthermore, unlike younger boys for whom physical aggression is often associated with social rejection, older *tough boys* who engage in physical aggression in the form of bullying are relatively popular among both boys and girls (Juvonen & Graham, 2014; Olweus, 2013). This would be expected from an evolutionary perspective as social dominance hierarchies become established (Geary, 2010, 2015). In sum, since males engage much more frequently and with more vigor and greater zest in play fighting than females, it follows that they can be far more easily socialized than females into antisocial forms of real fighting.

Biological Basis

Greater male exposure to prenatal testosterone provides a biological explanation for the sex difference in R&T. As described by Hines (2011, 2015), at 6–7 weeks prenatally the Sry (sex-region determining) gene on the Y chromosome induces differentiation of neutral gonads into testes. In the absence of the Sry gene, and with involvement of other genes, neutral gonads develop into ovaries at about 12 weeks. The testes begin to produce testosterone prenatally, whereas ovaries do not. This sex difference appears to be maximal between 8 and 24 weeks and then tapers off by birth. There is also a surge of testosterone during early postnatal development for males, peaking at about one to three months and declining to minimal levels at about 6 months where it remains until puberty. The relationship between testosterone prenatally and the postnatal surge is unknown (Kung, Browne, Constantinescu, Noorderhaven, & Hines, 2016).

Although studies examining the effects of the postnatal surge on male neurobehavioral development are just beginning to emerge (Hines, Spencer, Browne, Constantinescu, & Noorderhaven, 2016), there are thousands of studies across numerous species ranging from rodents to non-human primates showing unequivocally that sex hormones have organizational effects because they produce permanent changes to brain structures and the behaviors these structures subserve, including R&T and aggression (Berenbaum & Beltz, 2011; Hines, 2011, 2015; Hines, Constantine, & Spencer, 2015). The experimental nature of animal studies makes it possible to rule out psychosocial environmental confounds, an ever-present source of ambiguity in human studies.

The most extensively studied "natural experiment" on the effects of testosterone on human behavior is congenital adrenal hyperplasia (CAH). These studies provide the strongest evidence for a prenatal sex difference in testosterone on human behavior (Hines et al., 2016). This is an autosomal genetic recessive disorder that occurs in approximately 1:5000 to 1:15,000 male and female births, which results in increased production of androgen from the adrenal gland. Among females, exposure to excess androgen beginning early in gestation has many of the same effects as testosterone produced naturally by the testes among males during gestation. Although girls with CAH are typically born with partially virilized genitalia (Pasterski, Golombok, & Hines, 2011; Hines, 2013), there are rare cases when genital virilization is so severe that girls were mistaken for boys and reared as such (Hines, 2013). Nowadays, the disorder is typically diagnosed at birth, and girls are surgically feminized during infancy, reared as female, and provided ongoing medical treatment to prevent further virilization (Berenbaum & Belz, 2011). Findings in which CAH females are followed parallel those from research on testosterone among animals. In over a dozen studies from several independent research groups in several different countries, CAH girls show increased male-typical toy, playmate, and activity preferences (Hines et al., 2015). Furthermore, CAH girls exhibit more R&T and more physical aggression compared with their non-affected sisters and unrelated girls who are matched on age and SES (Berenbaum & Belz, 2011; Hines, 2011, 2015; Pasterski et al., 2011; Wong, Pasterski, Hindmarsh, Geffner, & Hines, 2013).[7]

Although these data provide support for the influence of the sex difference in prenatal androgen exposure on R&T, there remains a potential confounding influence of parental socialization in humans. If parents treat their CAH daughters differently because of girls' genital virilization at birth, this difference in parental treatment rather than exposure to androgen could explain at least some of the more male-typical behavior of CAH girls (Wong et al., 2013). However, three lines of research argue against this interpretation. First, severity of CAH in females is correlated positively with masculine behaviors. Furthermore, because genitalia of CAH girls are typically not completely virilized, their prenatal androgen exposure tends to be less extensive than that of a typical boy (Pasterski et al., 2011). Thus, their behavior might be even more masculinized if their exposure was the same as boys. Second, normal variability in maternal testosterone during pregnancy correlates with greater male typical play in non-CAH females. Finally, although parents report encouraging less girl-typical and more boy-typical toy play in CAH girls, this differential parental socialization is, at least in part, a response to their daughter's increased interest in masculine play (Wong et al., 2013).

[7] Because adult men have more circulating testosterone it is widely assumed that this difference contributes to men's higher level of aggression. However, correlations between testosterone and aggressive behavior in men are small, and thus it has not been possible to empirically demonstrate this effect (Hines, 2015).

Emotionality

Emotionality describes intensive and temporal variations in emotion expression (Stifter & Dollar, 2016). Emotionality includes both positive and negative emotionality, with the later historically receiving most of the research focus because of its relevance to understanding the development of both internalizing and externalizing disorders[8] (Stifter & Dollar, 2016). Negative emotionality is a temperament construct that includes the emotions of frustration/anger, hostility, irritability, sadness, guilt, discomfort, anticipatory anxiety and fear (DeLisi & Vaughn, 2014; Stifter & Dollar, 2016). Although the negative emotions of anger, hostility, and irritability have been most commonly associated with increased risk for antisocial behavior (DeLisi & Vaughn, 2014; Krieger & Stringaris, 2016), it is fear[9] that is most germane for understanding the sex difference in antisocial behavior, as a meta-analysis of sex differences in temperament in children (ages 3 months to 13 years) found no differences for any of the negative emotions other than fear (et al., 2006). This finding was affirmed once again 6 years later by the lead author of the meta-analysis (Else-Quest, 2012). In defining fear, it is important to note that it is not a unitary construct but has two components: threat reactivity which involves unconscious, automatic bodily reactions to imminent threat and the conscious experience of that threat (Hoppenbrouwers, Bulten, & Brazil, 2016).

Vulnerability

Temperamental fear is negatively associated with the development of antisocial behavior, with, for example, infants' expression of fear in the laboratory predicting lower maternal reports of aggression when the children

[8] Beginning with the work of Achenbach (1978), there is a commonly accepted distinction in developmental psychopathology between "externalizing" and "internalizing" disorders (Beauchaine & Hinshaw, 2013). Externalizing behavior disorders refer to a grouping of behavior problems that are manifested in children's outward behavior and reflect the child negatively acting on the *external* environment through disruptive, hyperactive, and aggressive behaviors. In contrast, *internalizing* behavior problems more centrally affect the child's internal psychological environment rather than the external world and are manifested in withdrawn, anxious, inhibited, and depressed behaviors.

[9] Although the difference between fear and anxiety has long been debated, there appears to be at least one core defining difference. Namely, fear involves a surge of physiological reactivity in response to clear and impending danger, whereas anxiety is a more diffuse emotion in which the threat is less certain and arousal is sustained, even after the removal of the threat (Hoppenbrouwers, Bulten, & Brazil, 2016).

were 7 years old (Stifter & Dollar, 2016). Moreover, there is "overwhelming evidence" (Raine, 2013, p. 117) for a *fear deficit* in antisocial individuals, especially psychopaths (Hoppenbrouwers et al., 2016). However, as reviewed by Hoppenbrouwers and colleagues (2016), this deficit, at least with regard to psychopathy, is primarily in threat reactivity The evidence for reduced subjective experience of fear is far less compelling, though it is possible that the deficiency in threat reactivity indirectly leads to less intensive conscious experiences. The different explanations for how the fear deficit results in a vulnerability include impairments in the appropriate processing and responding to both threats and distress in others, and a weak defensive system, the consequence of which is that behavioral avoidance is less likely to occur in the presence of environmental cues signaling danger. With regard to the latter explanation, since moral socialization is partly dependent upon negative arousal (i.e., fear) evoked by potential punishment, a diminished fearful inhibition will make it more difficult for a child to internalize societal norms (Krieger & Stringaris, 2016).

Sex Difference

There is a considerable body of work indicating that women, beginning in childhood, are more fearful than men (Campbell, 2013). There is a small sex difference in fear among children, evident in infancy, with girls being more fearful than boys (d = 0.12; Chaplin & Aldao, 2013; Else-Quest, 2012; Else-Quest et al., 2006). Evidence for this difference is based mainly on parent reports of their children's distress or withdrawal from sudden changes or novelty (Chaplin & Aldao, 2013). This difference increases from kindergarten through 6th grade, when girls are twice as likely as boys to be rated by teachers (17.4% vs. 8.6%) as fearful (i.e., "fearful or afraid of new things; is worried, worries about many things; cries easily"; Cote, Tremblay, Nagin, Zoccolillo, & Vitaro, 2002). By adolescence and continuing into adulthood, the sex difference increases to d = 0.40 (Else-Quest, 2012), when women are twice as likely as men to have a phobia (APA, 2013). This difference is even larger for situations that pose physical threats to bodily integrity, the type of fear most relevant to avoiding physical aggression (Campbell, 2013; 2016; Campbell & Cross, 2012).

Biological Basis

Low resting heart rate (LHR), a measure of autonomic hypoarousal, is an unequivocal risk factor for antisocial behavior in females as well as males, and in juveniles as well as adults (Raine, 2015). Importantly, this finding appears to be specific to antisocial behavior as it has not been found to be linked to other disorders such as anxiety, depression, schizophrenia (Portnoy et al., 2014). When measured in childhood, LHR predicts both adolescent conduct problems and violence (APA, 2013; Murray et al., 2015; Portnoy et al., 2012). Indeed, a systematic review a meta-analysis of resting heart rate and antisocial behavior found that LHR coincided with a 22% increase in violence (Portnoy & Farrington, 2015) which the authors remarked was "quite a substantial effect' (p. 40). Most recently, in an exceptional study based on data on 710, 264 Swedish men, Latvala, Kuja-Halkola, Almquist, Larsson, and Lichtenstein (2015) found that LHR at age 18 predicted a 49% increased risk for adult violence more than 30 years later, after taking into account multiple confounding factor. In sum, LHR is a robust biological correlate of antisocial behavior which can be interpreted as One interpretation of this finding is that LHR reflecting diminished threat reactivity (Portnoy et al., 2013; Raine, 2013). Furthermore, beginning at age 3 years, a sex difference emerges, with boys having lower resting heart rates than girls, by approximately 6.1 beats per second ($d = 0.36$) (Raine, 2013). The emergence of this difference at such an early age would seem to render far less likely an interpretation that a physiological adaptation to differential exposure to social adversity (see Choy et al., 2015), rather than an innate biological difference, might explain the LHR.

EMPATHY

Temperamental fear and empathy are very closely related as empathy can be conceptualized as an adaptive behavior which includes social responses to various emotional expressions such as pain and fear (Vachon, Lynam, & Johnson, 2013). Without fearful inhibition, it is more difficult for children to develop moral socialization, empathy and guilt (Krieger & Stringaris, 2016), and children high in temperamental fear have been shown to demonstrate better internalization of rules as well as showing more empathy/guilt (Stifter & Dollar, 2016). Empathy is generally viewed as having two forms (Vachon et al., 2013). Cognitive empathy is the ability to detect or understand emotions, whereas affective empathy is a visceral response that stems from comprehension of another's emotional state or condition, and is identical or very similar to what the other person is feeling or would be expected to feel (Eisenberg, Fabes, & Spinrad, 2006).

Vulnerability

It is commonly accepted that a deficit in affective empathy is a vulnerability to development of antisocial behavior, since individuals with such a deficit may not be deterred from such behaviors by expressions of distress by victims (Campbell & Cross, 2012; Raine, 2013; Vachon et al., 2013). However, a recent meta-analysis challenges this assumption (Vachon et al., 2013). In fact, the relationship between empathy and various forms of aggression (verbal, sexual, physical) is surprisingly weak. For example, empathy and physical aggression are only slightly correlated, $r = -0.12$. Nevertheless, the true relationship between empathy and aggression may be stronger if empathy is reconceptualized to include more maladaptive, clinical manifestations of callous disregard for the feelings of others and lack of remorse for the misery caused by one's actions (Vachon et al., 2013). This suggestion is consistent with the well characterized between relationship of what is alternatively termed *low prosociality* (Trentacosta & Goodlett, 2015) or *callous-unemotional* (CU) traits (e.g., lack of guilt/remorse, callous lack of empathy for the feelings of others) and serious conduct problems among juveniles (Goldmaryami & Frick, 2016). Indeed, among juveniles with severe conduct problems, those with elevated CU traits are at higher risk for severe and persistent antisocial outcomes, even after controlling for severity of conduct problems, age of onset, and common comorbid conditions (Frick & Ray, 2015; Goldmaryami & Frick, 2016). Thus, an extremely low level of empathy confers vulnerability to antisocial behaviors.

Sex Difference

Boys are more likely than girls to exhibit low levels on various measures of empathy in general, and on measures of the lowest levels of empathy as indexed by CU traits. With regard to empathy in general, reviews by Zahn-

Waxler et al. (2008) and Geary (2010) indicate that male newborns are less responsive to social stimuli and less able to make eye contact than female newborns. Girls 12 to 20 months old respond to the distress of other people with greater empathic concern than boys. Preschool girls, who are more socially aware than infants, exhibit more (a) empathy and prosociality, (b) social skills, (c) remorse after transgression, and (d) understanding of others' emotions, problems, and intentions than boys. Greater social sensitivity of girls continues throughout childhood and adolescence. Meta-analytic reviews of sex differences in empathy indicate a medium effect size ($d = 0.60$) favoring girls on self-reports (Eisenberg et al., 2006) and a small effect size (Hedges' $g = 0.13$) favoring girls on observational measures of facial, vocal, and behavioral expression (Olino, Durbin, Klein, Hayden, & Dyson, 2013. Following from these findings, Baron-Cohen (2003, 2011; Baron-Cohen et al., 2014) advanced an *Empathizing-Systemizing* theory of sex differences, which proposes that on average females have a stronger brain-based drive to *empathize* than males, and that males on average have a stronger drive to *systemize* (to analyze or construct rule-based systems). With regard to CU traits, boys score higher than girls on various measures from preschool to adolescence (Essau, Sasagawa, & Frick, 2006; Ezpeleta, Osa, Granero, Penelo, & Domenech, 2013; Frick, Bodin, & Barry, 2000; Frick, personal communication, September 2, 2013; Humayun, Kahn, Frick, & Viding, 2014; Rowe et al., 2010). For example, in a large sample of 3687 seven-year-old twin pairs representative of the population in the United Kingdom, 73% of boys versus 27% of girls were rated high on CU traits as assessed by teacher report (Humayun et al., 2014).

Biological Basis

Baron-Cohen has proposed that the male fetus's higher level of prenatal testosterone organizes the brain toward stronger systemizing and weaker empathy (Baron-Cohen 2003, 2011; Baron-Cohen et al., 2014). Evidence for this theory comes from the Cambridge Fetal Testosterone Project (n = 635), in which amniotic fluid obtained through amniocentesis is examined for testosterone. Among children who were followed up through age 11, higher levels of fetal testosterone were correlated with lower frequency of eye contact at 12 months, poorer quality of social relationships at 48 months, and diminished empathy at 48 and 96 months (Baron-Cohen et al., 2014).

Small Temperamental Sex Difference = Large Effect on Antisocial Behavior

A small sex difference in a temperamental trait can cause a large difference in antisocial behavior over time through two mechanisms: temperament–environment interplay and temperament x temperament interaction. The following section will discuss these mechanisms along with an example illustrating their operation.

Temperament-Environment Interplay

Temperament environment interplay refers to temperament–environment correlation and temperament x environment interaction (Plomin, DeFries, Knopik, & Neiderhiser, 2012). Temperament–environment correlation describes processes through which an individual's temperament influences his or her exposure to certain risky environments. Two forms, *active* and *evocative*, explain how small sex difference may cause a large difference in antisocial behavior over time. In the *active* process, a child with an impulsive temperament may actively seek out risky experiences and environments (e.g., association with deviant peers) and thus increase the likelihood of engaging in an antisocial behavior such as illegal substance use (Beauchaine & Gatzke-Kopp, 2013; Krieger & Stringaris, 2016). In the *evocative* process, a child's impulsive temperament increases the likelihood of evoking negative interactions from others, thereby increasing the probability of engaging in oppositional/defiant behavior. For example, it is estimated that a typical child with ADHD engages in an astonishing half a million negative interchanges each year (Pelham & Fabiano, 2008). This process is especially pernicious in contexts where the parenting figures are themselves antisocial and thus prone to engage in harsh/punitive parenting practices (DeLisi & Vaughn, 2014). Thus, an initially small difference early in life may "snowball" during development, creating larger and larger phenotypic effects (Plomin et al., 2012).

Temperament-environment interaction refers to processes in which the effects of the environment on antisocial behavior depend on or are moderated by temperament (Beauchaine & Gatzke-Kopp, 2013; Krieger & Stringaris, 2016). Note that when temperament-environment interaction is operative, individuals are not actively choosing or evoking environments but rather have a temperamental vulnerability that renders them more susceptible to the risky environment in which they find themselves (Krieger & Stringaris, 2016). The paradigmatic example of such an interaction is the previously mentioned Caspi and colleagues study (2002) which was the first recorded instance in the behavioral sciences of an interaction which identified a genetic susceptibility (MAOA-L) to an environmental exposure (maltreatment) (Moffitt, 2005).

In this study there was the remarkable finding that although the vulnerability per se did not confer a risk for antisocial behavior (no main effect), males with the *MAOA-L* genotype who experienced maltreatment and who comprised only 12% of the sample, accounted for an astounding 44% of violent convictions.

Temperament x Temperament Interaction

Temperament x temperament interaction refer to process by which one temperamental trait moderates the association between another temperamental trait and a child's psychopathology, e.g., antisocial behavior (Stifter & Dollar, 2016). Hence, because temperamental vulnerabilities, although they may occur in isolation, frequently co-occur (Krieger & Stringaris, 2016), temperament x temperament interactions should be quite common. However, there is relatively little research on these interactions, with the bulk of the limited research involving low EC/impulsivity and other temperaments, especially negative emotionality (DeLisi & Vaughn, 2014, 2015; Stifter & Dollar, 2016). The interaction most relevant to explaining the sex difference in antisocial behavior (especially psychopathy) is between low EC and low fear/empathy (Krieger & Stringaris, 2016). Children with these vulnerabilities can be expected to be "challenging to supervise" and likely to produced "interpersonal friction" compared to children without these vulnerabilities (DeLisi & Vaughn, 2014, p.15).

In sum, since temperamental vulnerabilities frequently co-occur, a child who has more than one vulnerability trait faces a potential cascade of interactive effects with adverse environments. The cumulative impact of these interactive effects may be synergistic and thus yield a larger effect on the sex difference in antisocial behavior than would be expected from a simple additive effect of multiple vulnerabilities (Evans, Li, & Whipple, 2013; Masten & Cicchetti, 2010; Neuhaus & Beauchaine, 2013).

Conclusion

Although temperamental traits, which refer to biologically based early-developing behavioral and emotional tendencies, have long been understood to be important constructs for understanding normal and abnormal development, their relevance to criminal justice has only recently been recognized. This paper extended belated recognition to an examination of how sex differences in temperament, in interplay with one another as well as with numerous environmental risk factors, contribute to the massive sex difference in the severest forms of antisocial behavior.

A sex difference in at least three broad temperamental dimensions was identified. The dimensions involve attention/regulation processes, activity level, and emotionality. A sex difference on these dimensions results in males being more likely to be behaviorally and emotionally impulsive, being more easily socialized into physical aggression, and being less fearful and empathic and therefore less likely to internalize rules. A plausible biological mechanism mediating each of these sex differences was also discussed.

Future Research Directions

Since an "article of faith in criminology is that prevention offers the greatest potential for crime reduction" (DeLisi & Vaughn, 2014, p.19), the single most important direction for research should be the translation of findings on sex differences on temperamental traits into implications for early intervention. All the more so since to date very few interventions focused on temperament have been conducted with aim of reducing emotional and antisocial disorders (Stifter & Dollar, 2016). More specifically and perforce briefly, of the temperamental traits that have been examined, this paper would argue that the identification and treatment of ADHD in preschool children should assume primary importance for three reasons. First, as previously discussed, a deficit in self-control (with ADHD being the paradigmatic disorder of self-control) is arguably, if not indisputably, the single most important variable in explaining developmental origins of antisocial behavior. Second, it is now clear that diagnostic criteria for ADHD (especially combined presentation) can be used validly for 4-6 year-old children, with most children so diagnosed have an increased risk for functional impairment into adolescence (Lahey et al., 2016). Third, both pharmacological (Greenhill et al.,

2006) and psychosocial interventions with children and parents (Webster-Stratton, Reid, & Beauchaine, 2013) are efficacious treatments for ADHD in the short term. However, long-term benefits of such early interventions have yet to be demonstrated (Gleason, 2013), as is true for other interventions that target temperament-specific factors that relate to antisocial behavior (DeLisi & Vaughn, 2014).

Indeed, to state the obvious, preventing crime is "hard work" (Welsh & Farrington, 2013, p. 448) and thus there is pressing need to "redouble" efforts, especially as it relates in early intervention (Gleason, 2013, p. 229).

REFERENCES

Achenbach T. (1978). The child behavior profile: I. Boys aged 6–11. *Journal of Consulting and Clinical Psychology, 46*, 478–488.

American Psychiatric Association (2013). *Diagnostic and statistical manual of mental disorders, 5th edition*. Washington, DC: American Psychiatric Publishing.

Archer, J. (2004). Sex differences in aggression real-world settings: A meta-analytic review. *Review of General Psychology, 8,* 291−322.

Archer, J. (2009). Does sexual selection explain human sex differences in aggression? *Behavior and Brain sciences, 32,* 249 – 311.

Arnett, A., Pennington, B., Willcutt, E., DeFries, J., & Olson, R. (2015). Sex differences in ADHD symptom severity. *Journal of Child Psychology and Psychiatry, 56*, 632-639.

Baron-Cohen, S., Lombardo, M., Auyeung, B., Ashwin, E., Chakraharti, B., & Knickmeyer, R. (2014). Why is autism more common in males? In V. Hu (Ed.), *Frontiers in autism research: new horizons for diagnosis and treatment* (pp. 451-470). New Jersey: World Scientific.

Bates, J., Schermerhorn, A., & Petersen, I. (2014). *Temperament concepts in developmental psychopathology*. In M. Lewis and K. Rudolph (Eds.), (3rd ed., pp. 311-329). New York: Springer.

Beauchaine, T., & McNulty, T. (2013). Comorbidities and continuities as ontogenic processes: Toward developmental spectrum model of externalizing behavior. *Development and Psychopathology, 25*, 1505–1527.

Beauchaine, T., Shader, T., & Hinshaw, S. (2016). An ontogenic processes model of externalizing psychopathology. In T. Beauchaine & S. Hinshaw

(Eds.), *The Oxford handbook of externalizing spectrum disorders* (485-502). New York: Oxford University Press.

Beaver, K., & Connolly, E. (2015). Key findings from biosocial research and what they mean for the future of criminology. In M. DeLisi & M. Vaughn (Eds.), *The Routledge international handbook of biosocial criminology* (pp. 46-56). New York: Routledge.

Beaver, K. & Nedelec, J. (2015). A biological explanation for the male-female differences in criminal involvement. In K. Beaver, J. Barnes, & B. Boutwell (Eds.), *The nurture vs. biosocial debate in criminology* (pp. 25-40). Los Angeles: Sage.

Berenbaum, S., & Beltz, A. (2011). Sexual differentiation of human behavior: Effects of prenatal and pubertal organizational hormones. *Frontiers in Neuroendocrinology, 32*, 183-200.

Blakemore, J., Berenbaum, S., & Liben, L. (2008). *Gender development.* New York: Psychology Press.

Buss, D. (2012). *Evolutionary psychology: The new science of the mind* (4th ed.). New York: Allyn & Bacon.

Byrd, A., & Manuck, S. (2014). M*AOA*, childhood maltreatment, and antisocial behavior: Meta-analysis of a gene-environment interaction. *Biological Psychiatry*, *75*, 9–17.

Campbell, A. (2013). The evolutionary psychology of women's aggression. *Philosophical Transactions of the Royal Society B, 368,* 1-11.

Campbell, A. (2016). Women's competition and aggression. In D. Buss (Ed.), *The handbook of evolutionary psychology* (2nd ed., Vol. 2, pp. 684-703). Hoboken, NJ: Wiley.

Campbell, A., & Cross, C. (2012). Women and aggression. In T. Shackelford & V. Weekes-Schackelford (Eds.), *The Oxford handbook on evolutionary perspectives on violence, homicide and war* (pp. 197-217). New York: Oxford University Press.

Campo, N., Chamaerlain, S., Sahakian, B., & Robbins, T. (2011). The roles of dopamine and noradrenaline in the pathophysiology and treatment of Attention-Deficit/Hyperactivity Disorder. *Biological Psychiatry, 69,* e145-e157.

Caspi, A., McClay, J., Moffitt, T., Mill, J., Martin, J., & Craig, I. (2002). Role of genotype in the cycle of violence in maltreated children. *Science, 297*, 851–853.

Castellanos-Ryan, N. & Sequin, N. (2016). Prefrontal and anterior cingulated cortex mechanisms of impulsivity. In T. Beauchaine & S. Hinshaw (Eds.),

The Oxford handbook of externalizing spectrum disorders (201-219). New York: Oxford University Press.

Chaplin, T., & Aldao, A. (2013). Gender difference in emotion expression in children: A meta-analytic review. *Psychological Bulletin, 139*, 735-765.

Chen, X. & Schmidt, L. (2015). Temperament and personality. In M. Lamb & R. Lerner (Eds.), *Handbook of child psychology and developmental science,* (7th ed., vol. 3, pp. 152-200). New York: Wiley.

Choy, O., Raine, A., Portnoy, J., Rudo-Hutt, A., Gao, Y., & Soyfer, L. (2015). The mediating role of heart rate on the social-adversity-antisocial relationship: a social neurocriminology perspective. *Journal of Research in Crime and Delinquency, 52,* 303-341.

Cote, S., Tremblay, R., Nagin, D., Zoccolillo, M., & Vitaro, F. (2002). The development of impulsivity, fearfulness, and helpfulness during childhood: patterns of consistency and change in the trajectories of boys and girls. *Journal of Child Psychology and Psychiatry, 43*, 609-618.

Cross, C., Copping, L., & Campbell, A. (2011). Sex differences in impulsivity: A meta-analysis. *Psychological Bulletin, 137*, 97-130.

Da Silva, D. Rijo, D., & Salekin, R. (2015). The evolutionary roots of psychopathy. *Aggression and Violent Behavior, 21,* 85-96.

Del Giudice, M., & Ellis, B. (2016). Evolutionary foundations of developmental psychopathology. In D. Cicchetti (Ed.), *Developmental psychopathology* (*3rd* ed., Vol 2., pp.1-58). New York: Wiley.

DeLisi, M., & Vaughn, M. (2014). Foundation for a temperament-based theory of antisocial behavior and criminal justice system involvement. *Journal of Criminal Justice, 42,* 10-25.

Diamond, A. (2013). Executive functions. *Annual review of psychology, 64*, 135-168. Dorfman, H., & Buckholtz, J. (2015). Neuogenetics of antisocial aggression. In M. DeLisi & M. Vaughn, (Eds.), *The Routledge international handbook of biosocial criminology* (115-127). New York: Routledge.

Eisenberg, N. Edwards, A., Spinrad, T., Salquist, J., Eggum, N., & Reiser, M. (2013). Are effortful control and reactive control unique constructs in young children? *Developmental Psychology, 49*, 2028-2094.

Eisner, M., & Malti, T. (2015). Aggressive and violent behavior. In M. Lamb & R. Lerner (Eds.), *Handbook of child psychology and developmental science,* (7th ed., vol. 3, pp. 795-841). New York: Wiley.

Else-Quest, N., Hyde, J., Goldsmith, H., & Van Hulle, C. (2006). Gender differences in temperament: A meta-analysis. *Psychological Bulletin, 132,* 33–72.

Else-Quest, N. (2012). Gender differences in temperament. In M. Zenter & R. Shiner (Eds.), *Handbook of temperament* (pp. 479-496). New York: The Guildford Press.

Eme, R. (2013). MAOA and male antisocial behavior: A review. *Aggression and Violent Behavior, 18,* 395-398.

Eme, R. (2014). Is serious physical violence almost exclusively male? *Violence and Gender, 1*, 90-93.

Frick, P., & Ray, J. (2015). Evaluating callous-unemotional traits as a personality construct. *Journal of Personality, 83,* 710-722.

Geary, D. (2010). *Male, female: the evolution of human sex differences* (2nd ed.). Washington DC: American Psychological Association.

Geary, D. (2015). *Evolution of vulnerability: implications for sex differences in health and development.* New York: Academic Press.

Gleason, M. (2013). Finding the tools for effective early intervention for preschool Attention-Deficit/Hyperactivity Disorder. *Journal of the American Academy of Child and Adolescent Psychiatry, 52,* 228-230.

Goldman, D., & Rosser, A. (2014). MAOA-environment interactions. Results may vary. *Biological Psychiatry*, *75*, 2–3.

Goldmaryami, F., & Frick, P. (2016). Callous-unemotional traits and the development of externalizing spectrum disorders. In T. Beauchaine & S. Hinshaw (Eds.), *The Oxford handbook of externalizing spectrum disorders* (360-374). New York: Oxford University Press.

Greenhill, L., Kollins, S., Abikoff, H., McCracken, J., Riddle, M., & Swanson, J. (2006). Efficacy and safety of immediate-release methylphenidate treatment for preschoolers with ADHD. *Journal of the American Academy of Child and Adolescent Psychiatry, 45*, 1284-1293.

Halpern, D. (2012). *Sex differences in cognitive abilities* 4th ed.). New York: Psychology Press.

Hines, M. (2011). Gender development and the human brain. *Annual review of neuroscience, 34*, 69-88.

Hines, M. (2013). Sex and sex differences. In P. Zelazo (Ed.), *The Oxford handbook of developmental psychology* (Vol. 1., pp. 164-201). New York: Oxford University Press.

Hines, M. (2015). Gendered development. In M. Lamb & R. Lerner (Eds.), *Handbook of child psychology and developmental science,* (7th ed., vol. 3, pp. 842-887). New York: Wiley.

Hines, M., Constantinescu, M., & Spencer, D., (2015). Early androgen exposure and human gender development. *Biology of Sex Differences, 6,* 1-10.

Hines, M., Spencer, D., Browne, W., Constantinescu, M., & Noorderhaven, R. (2016). The early post-natal period, mini-puberty, provides a window on the role of testosterone in human neurobehavioural development. *Current Opinion in Neurobiology, 38,* 69-73.

Holden, C. (2005). Sex and the suffering brain. *Science, 308,* 1574−1577.

Holz, N., Boecker, R., Buchmann, A., Bloomeyer, D., Baumeister, S., Hohmann, S., Jennen-Steinmetz, C., Laucht, M. (2016). Evidence for a sex-dependent MAOA x childhood stress interaction in the neural circuitry of aggression. *Cerebral Cortex, 26,* 904-914.

Hoppenbrouwers, S., Bulten, B., & Brazil, I. (2016). Parsing fear: a reassessment of the evidence for fear deficits in psychopathy. *Psychological Bulletin,* Advance online publication.

Ingalhalikar, M., Smith, A., Parker, D., Satterthwaite, T., Elliott, M., Ruparel, K., Verma, R. (2014). Sex difference in the structural connectome of the human brain. *Proceedings of the National Academy of Sciences*, *14,* 823-828.

Juvonen, J., & Graham, S. (2014). Bullying in schools: The power of bullies and the plight of their victims. *Annual Review of Psychology*, 65, 159-185.

Kagan, J. (2013). Behavioral inhibition as a temperamental vulnerability to psychopathology. In T. Beauchaine & S. Hinshaw (Eds.), *Child and adolescent psychopathology* (2nd ed., pp. 227-250). Hoboken NJ: Wiley.

Kim-Cohen, J., Caspi, A., Taylor, A., Williams, B., Newcombe, R., Craig, I., & Moffitt, T. E. (2006). MAOA maltreatment, and gene–environment interaction predicting children's mental health: New evidence and a meta-analysis. *Molecular Psychiatry, 11*, 903–913.

Krieger, F., & Stringaris, A. (2016). Temperament and vulnerability to externalizing behaviors. In T. Beauchaine & S. Hinshaw (Eds.), *The Oxford handbook of externalizing spectrum disorders* (pp. 170-183). New York: Oxford University. Press.

Kung, K., Browne, W., Constantinescu, M., Noorderhaven, R., & Hines, M. (2016). Early postnaral testosterone predicts sex-related differences in early expressive vocabulary. *Psychoendocrinology, 68,* 111-116.

Lahey, B., Sibley, M., Molina, B., Lee, S., Applegate, B., & Pelham, W. (2016). Predictors of adolescent outcomes among 4-6 year-old children with Attention-Deficit/Hyperactivity Disorder. *Journal of Abnormal Child Psychology, 125,* 168-181.

Lai, M., Lombardo, M., Auyeung, B., Chakrabarti, B., & Baron-Cohen, S. (2015). Sex/Gender differences and autism: setting the scene for future research. *Journal of the American Academy of Child and Adolescent Psychiatry, 54,* 11-24.

Latvala, A., Kuja-Halkola, R., Almquist, C., Larsson, H., & Lichtenstein, P. (2015). A longitudinal study of resting heart rate and violent criminality in more than 700,000 men. *JAMA Psychiatry, 72,* 971-978.

Maccoby, E. (1998). *The two sexes growing up apart, coming together.* Cambridge, MA: The Belknap Press of Harvard University Press.

Martel, M. (2013). Sexual selection and sex differences in the prevalence of childhood externalizing and adolescent internalizing disorder. *Psychological Bulletin, 139,* 1221-1259.

Martel, M., Gremillion, M., & Tackett, J. (2014). Personality traits elucidate sex differences in Attention-Deficit/Hyperactivity Disorder comorbidity during early childhood. *Journal of Psychopathology and Behavior Assessment, 36*, 237-245.

McClelland, M., Geldhof, G., Cameron, C., & Wanless, S. (2015). Development and self-regulation. In W. Overton & P. Molenaar (Eds.), *Handbook of child psychology and developmental science* (7th ed., vol 1., pp. 523-565). New York: Wiley.

Moffitt, T. (2005). The new look of behavioral genetics in developmental psychopathology: Gene–environment interplay in antisocial behavior. *Psychological Bulletin, 131,* 533–554.

Moffitt, T. (2012). Self-control, then and now. In R. Loeber & B. Welsch (Eds.), *The future of criminology* (pp. 40-45). New York: Oxford University Press.

Moffitt, T. Arseneault, L., Belsky, D., Dickson, N., Hancox, R. Harrington, H., Houtts, R. Caspi, A. (2011). A gradient of childhood self-control predicts health, wealth, and public safety. *Proceedings of the National Academy of Sciences of the United States of America, 108*, 2693-2698.

Murray, J., Hallal, P., Mielke, G., Raine, A., Wehrmeister, F., Anselm, J., & Barros, F. (2015). Low resting heart rate is associated with violence in late adolescence: a prospective birth cohort study in Brazil. *International Journal of Epidemiology* National Institute of Mental Health (2015). Strategic plan for research.

Nigg, J. (2006). Temperament and developmental psychopathology. *Journal of Child Psychology and Psychiatry, 4*, 395-422.

Nigg, J. (2016). Attention and impulsivity. In D. Cicchetti (Ed.). *Developmental psychopathology*: *Risk, disorder and adaptation* (3rd ed., vol 3., pp. 591-646). New York: Wiley.

Olweus, D. (2013). School bullying: Development and some important challenges. *Annual review of clinical psychology, 9*, 14.1-14.3.

Ouellet-Morin, I., Cote, S., Vitaro, F., Herbert, M., Carbonneau, R., Lacourse, E., Turecki, G., Tremblay, R. (2016). Effects of the MAOA gene and levels of exposure to violence on antisocial outcomes. *The British Journal of Psychiatry, 208,* 42-48.

Parsch, J., & Ellegen, H. (2013). The evolutionary causes and consequences of sex-biased gene expression. *Nature Reviews Genetics, 14*, 83–87.

Pasterski, V., Golombok, S., & Hines, M. (2011). Sex differences in social behavior. In P. Smith & C. Hart (Ed.), *The Wiley-Blackwell handbook of childhood social development* (2nd ed., pp. 281-298). West Sussex, UK: Blackwell Publishing Ltd.

Pellis, S. & Pellis, V. (2011). Rough-and-tumble play: Training and using the social brain. In P. Nathan & A Pellegrini (Eds.), *The Oxford handbook of the development of play* (pp. 245-259). New York: Oxford University Press.

Pinker, S. (2011). *The better angels of our nature: why violence has declined.* New York: Penguin Group.

Portnoy, J., Chen, F., Gao, Y., Niv, S., Schug, R., Yang, Y., & Raine, A. (2014). Biological perspectives on sex differences in crime and antisocial behavior. In R. Gartner & B. McCarthy (Eds.), *Gender, sex and crime* (pp. 260-285).

Portnoy, J., & Farrington, D. (2015). Resting heart rate and antisocial behavior: an updated systematic review and meta-analysis. *Aggression and Violent Behavior, 22,* 33-45.

Portnoy, J. Gao, Y., Glenn, A., Niv, S., Peskin, M., Rudo-Hutt, A., Schug, R. Raine, A. (2012). The biology of childhood-crime and antisocial behavior. In C. Gibson & M. Krohn (Eds.), *Handbook of life-course criminology* (pp, 21-42). New York: Springer Science-Business Media.

Poulton, R., Moffitt, T., & Silva, P. (2015). The Dunnedin Multidisciplinary health and development study: overview of the first 40 years, with an eye to the future. *Social Psychiatry and Psychiatric Epidemiology, 50,* 679-673.

Raine, A. (2013). *The anatomy of violence: The biological roots of crime.* New York: Pantheon Books.

Raine, A. (2015). Low resting heart rate as an unequivocal risk factor for both the perpetration and exposure to violence. *JAMA Psychiatry, 72,* 942-964.

Robins, L. (1966). *Deviant children grown up: A sociological and psychiatric study of sociopathic personality*. Huntington New York: Robert E. Krieger Publishing Company.

Robins, L. (1978). Sturdy childhood predictors of adult antisocial behavior: replications from longitudinal studies. *Psychological Medicine, 8,* 611-622.

Rothbart, M. (2012). Advances in temperament: History, concepts, and measures. In M. Zenter & R. Shiner (Eds.), *Handbook of temperament* (pp. 3-20). New York: The Guildford Press.

Russell, M., Robins, S., & Odgers, C. (2014). Developmental perspectives: sex difference in antisocial behavior from childhood to adulthood. In R. Gartner & B. McCarthy (Eds.), *The Oxford handbook of gender, sex, and crime.* New York: Oxford University Press.

Sharma, L., Markon, K., & Clarke, L. (2014). Toward a theory of distinct types of "impulsive" behaviors: A meta-analysis of self-report and behavioral measures. *Psychological Bulletin, 140,* 374-408.

Stetler, D., Davis, C., Leavitt, K., Schriger, I., Benson, K., Bhaka, S., Wang, L., Bortolato, M. (2014). Association of low-activity MAOA allelic variations with violent crime in incarcerated offenders. *Journal of Psychiatric Research, 58,* 69-75.

Stewart, A., & McDermott, C. (2004). Gender in psychology. *Annual review of psychology, 55*, 519–554.

Stifter, C., & Dollar, J. (2016). Temperament and developmental psychopathology. In D. Cicchetti (Ed.), *Developmental psychopathology* (3rd ed., Vol. 4, pp. 546-607). New York: Wiley.

Tackett, J., Martel, M., & Kushner, S. (2012). Temperament, externalizing disorders, and Attention-Deficit/Hyperactivity Disorder. In M. Zenter & R. Shiner (Eds.), *Handbook of temperament* (pp. 562-579). New York: The Guildford Press.

Tiihonen, J., Rautianen, M., Ollila, O., Repo-Tiihonen, E., Virkunen, M., Palotie, A., Pietilainen, O., Paunio, T. (2015). Genetic background of extreme violent behavior. *Molecular Psychiatry, 20,* 786-792.

Tomasi, D., & Volkow, N. (2012a). Abnormal functional connectivity in children with attention-deficit/hyperactivity disorder. *Biological Psychiatry, 71*, 443-450.

Tomasi, D., & Volkow, N. (2012b). Gender differences in brain functional connectivity density. *Human Brain Mapping, 33*, 849-860.

Tremblay, R. (2010). Developmental origins of disruptive behavior problems: The 'original sin' hypothesis, epigenetics and their consequences for prevention. *Journal of Child Psychology and Psychiatry, 51,* 341 – 367.

Trentacosta, C., & Goodlett, B. (2015). Early dispositional risks for conduct problems and gene-environment interplay. In M. DeLisi & M. Vaughn (Eds.), *The Routledge international handbook of biosocial criminology* (pp. 403-417). New York: Routledge

Webster-Stratton, C., Reid, M., & Beauchaine, T. (2011). Combining parent and child training for young children with ADHD. *Journal of Clinical Child and Adolescent Psychology, 40,* 191-203.

Weeland, J., Overbeek, G., de Castro, B., & Matthys, W. (2015). Underlying mechanisms of gene-environment interactions in externalizing behavior: a systematic review and search for theoretical mechanisms. *Clinical Child and Family Psychology Review, 18,* 413-442.

Welsh, B., & Farrington, D. (2013). Preventing crime is hard work: developmental criminology, and the enduring legacy of James Q. Wilson. *Journal of Criminal Justice, 41,* 448-451.

Wong, W., Pasterski, V., Hindmarsh, P., Geffner, M., & Hines, M. (2013). Are there parental socialization effects on the sex-typed behavior of individuals with congenital adrenal hyperplasia? *Archives of Sexual Behavior*, *42*, 381–391.

Zisner, A., & Beauchaine, T. (2016). Midbrain neural mechanisms of trait impulsivity. In T. Beauchaine & S. Hinshaw (Eds.), *The Oxford handbook of externalizing spectrum disorders* (184-200). New York: Oxford University Press.

In: Antisocial Behavior ISBN: 978-1-53612-954-0
Editors: Abby Dobson and Peter Talbot © 2017 Nova Science Publishers, Inc.

Chapter 2

Antisocial Behavior and Resident Participation in Housing Management: A Study in Hong Kong's Private Housing Sector

***Yung Yau*[1,*] *and Shuk Man Chiu*[2]**
[1]Department of Public Policy, City University of Hong Kong, Kowloon, Hong Kong, China
[2]Independent Researcher, China

Abstract

The problem of antisocial behavior (ASB) or minor incivilities in housing has attracted extensive public attention in many jurisdictions. In spite of the deployment of various approaches, ranging from family intervention and probationary tenancies to statutory orders, the ASB problem still proliferates in most places. As suggested in the literature, ASB can result in reduced residential satisfaction, poor physical and mental health and social disruption. However, how ASB affects the decision or behavior of residents in housing management participation has been ignored in previous studies. Hypothetically, the impacts of ASB can influence resident participation in both directions. On one hand, residents tend to participate more actively in housing management when they cannot tolerate the ASB in their living places and want to make a

* Corresponding Author Email: y.yau@cityu.edu.hk.

change. On the other hand, proliferation of ASB problem may weaken the social tie and bonding within a residential neighborhood, leading to the dwindled willingness of the residents to participate in collective actions in housing management. This study aims to explore the link between residents' ASB perceptions and their levels of participation in housing management in private multi-owned housing (MOH) developments empirically. An analytic model illustrating how ASB perceptions can have a catalytic effect on resident participation in MOH management is developed. Based on the findings of a structured questionnaire survey on residents of private MOH in Hong Kong, the model was tested using a path-analytic technique. The analysis results show that ASB perceptions affect private housing residents' participation levels in MOH management. Policy recommendations then follow.

Keywords: antisocial behavior, multi-owned housing, collective actions, Hong Kong, housing management, path analysis

INTRODUCTION

The pursuit of a quality living environment is important to most people because housing quality has been found to significantly affect one's life quality (Raw and Hamilton, 1995; Dunn, 2000; Newcombe et al., 2005). Housing quality is a multi-facet concept. It depends on a wide range of factors including relatively fixed housing features such as location and physical configurations and easily changeable operational aspects like quality of housing management and residents' behavior (Wong et al., 2006). In many cities where multi-owned housing (MOH) is predominant, quality living environment is jeopardized by mismanagement of housing assets. Non-participation or inactivity of residents in housing governance is an oft-cited cause of mismanagement of MOH. It is because governance of MOH often necessitates collective actions among the residents and the free-rider problem prevails.

Meanwhile, the impacts of antisocial behavior (ASB) on living environment quality started gaining growing attention from policy-makers, housing authorities, academics and other stakeholders in the West in the 1980s. Serious problems of ASB have been encountered in many western countries. For example, in Australia, around 10% and 25% of the households reported illegal drugs and vandalism respectively in their neighborhoods (Australian Bureau of Statistics, 2006). In 2004, 12% of social housing tenants in Scotland reported having experienced a problem with their neighbor in the last 12 months (Glasgow Housing Association, 2007). In the United Kingdom as a whole, ASB cases reported to the public authorities amounted 13.5 million each year (Wood, 2004). The community in the United Kingdom generally ranked ASB as the top-priority agenda in the arena of crime and disorder fighting (Ipsos MORI, 2010). In the United States, around 25.4 million and 9.8 million dwellings are subject to neighborhood problems of noise and litter respectively (United States Census Bureau, 2010). In Hong Kong, 25% of public housing tenants found neighborhood problems in their estates were intolerable (Yau, 2011b). Yau (2012) reported that 34.5% of private housing residents found ASB problem intolerable in their living places.

On account of the proliferation of ASB in the country, the UK Government launched a public consultation on the new statutory control regime of ASB in August 2011 (Department for Communities and Local Government, 2011). Before that, other attempts like introductory or probationary tenancies, stricter tenancy enforcement (e.g., by means of lease termination) and statutory orders (e.g., ASB orders, injunction orders and parenting orders) have been adopted to deal with the problem. ASB has long been a hot issue in the policy arena because of its direct and indirect impacts on life quality of the whole community. Previous studies like Agyemang et al. (2007), Curtis et al. (2004) and Jacobson et al. (2008) found that ASB could result in reduced residential satisfaction, poor physical and mental health and social disruption.

However, ASB studies attract not much scholarly attention in the East while they are rather popular in the West. Moreover, no previous attempt has been made to explore if ASB proliferation is associated with non-participation of residents in housing management. In theory, ASB can affect resident participation in two directions. On one hand, when the ASB problem is too serious in a residential community and the residents there can no longer tolerate it, the residents may participate more actively in community collective actions like informal social control and housing management to counter the delinquency and improve their living environment. On the other hand, proliferation of ASB problem may weaken the social tie and bonding within a residential neighborhood, leading to the dwindled willingness of the residents to participate in housing management which is of collective-action nature in many cases. In this regard, this chapter aims to empirically investigate whether residents' perceptions of ASB seriousness in residential neighborhood catalyze or undermine their participation in housing management affairs in MOH developments in Hong Kong. Based on the findings of a structured questionnaire survey on private housing residents, correlation and path analyses are conducted. The analysis results show that a resident's participation level is indirectly dependent on his or her ASB perceptions, with the sense of community serving as a mediator.

This chapter is organized as follows. The nature and causes of ASB are first reviewed. It is then followed by a review of the impacts of ASB proliferation in residential communities. Afterwards, the design of an empirical study exploring the link between ASB perceptions and resident participation in MOH management is detailed. The analysis results of the empirical study and their policy implications are discussed before the chapter is concluded.

Antisocial Behavior: What and Why?

The term 'ASB' has been lacking a universally accepted definition (Millie, 2009). It is generally used interchangeably with other terms like 'quality of life issues,' 'minor disorder,' 'incivilities' and 'neighborhood problems.' Different parties define the term 'ASB' in their own ways for diverse purposes. For example, ASB was broadly described by South Kesteven District Council (2016) in the United Kingdom as "day-to-day incidents of nuisance and disorder that affects people's lives." On the other hand, Millie et al. (2005, p. 3) defined ASB, in a very detailed manner, as behavior that "causes harassment, alarm or distress to individuals not of the same household as the perpetrator, such that it requires interventions from the relevant authorities; but criminal prosecution and punishment may be inappropriate because individual components of the behavior are not prohibited by criminal law or in isolation constitute relative minor offences."

From above, it is quite clear that the definition of ASB can be rather elastic (Brown, 2004). Similarly, perceptions of ASB are determined by a batch of factors such as context, location, social norm and interpretation etc. (Mackenzie et al., 2010; Nixon et al., 2003). That means the behavior that is considered 'anti-social' to one person can be seen as acceptable to another. In general, ASB in the housing context generally denotes the unacceptable behavior of the residents or visitors that are classified as wrong-doings conducted in opposition to the society's norms and accepted standards of behavior (Chartered Institute of Housing, 1995). It can take different forms and covers noise nuisance, littering, uncontrolled dogs, graffiti, vandalism, abusive uses of communal space, harassment and intimidation.

The roots of ASB are multi-faceted. From the agency viewpoint, the problem can be attributed to family problems (e.g., early abuse and neglect), poor educational attainment, unemployment and substance abuse (Eysenck, 1996; Home Office, 2003; Kerig and Becker, 2015; Morizot, 2015). On the other hand, structuralists suggest that social forces like decline in moral and family values contribute to ASB proliferation in a society. Ipsos MORI (2006) and Jacobs and Arthurson (2003) named limited opportunities available for young people and poor parenting as major factors of ASB proliferation in the West. In addition to the agency and structural factors just discussed, poor design and planning of housing has been conceived a key contributor to the neighborhood problems in Australia (Jacobs and Arthurson, 2003).

Impacts of ASB Proliferation in Residential Communities

ASB is a big but thorny issue in housing or urban management. However, while the public and policy focus tend to be upon control of ASB, not much works have attended to the impacts of ASB on individuals and communities (Innes and Weston, 2010). ASB proliferation can create a negative image for a city or urban area, affecting tourism and many other walks of life (Deery and Jago, 2010). According to the 'broken windows' theory and so-called zero-tolerance doctrines of policies, failure to control these relatively minor incivilities in an area can lead to the proliferation of more serious crimes there (Innes, 1999; Wilson and Kelling, 1982). Numerous studies like LaGrange et al. (1992) and Perkins and Taylor (1996) established a link between a neighborhood's level of physical and social disorder (e.g., litter, graffiti and vandalism) and fear of crime. Perceptions of neighborhood quality will in turn predict depressive symptoms of the residents (Latkin and Curry, 2003). Latkin et al. (2005) presented a pathway of physical and social disorder in a neighborhood which led to psychological distress and drug injection behavior of the residents. Moreover, ASB can result in reduced residential satisfaction, poor physical and mental health and social disruption (Agyemang et al., 2007; Andersen, 2008; Curtis et al., 2004; Hope and Hough; 1988; Jacobson et al., 2008). From the economic perspective, prevalence of ASB in a neighborhood can pull down the values of the properties (Brown, 2011).

Nonetheless, nearly all previous studies on the impacts of ASB or minor incivilities were conducted in the West. Similar research focus has been largely ignored in the East. In addition, although some of the literature worked on the relationship between ASB and social interactions within a neighborhood, how ASB shapes people's participation in community collective actions (e.g., management of MOH development) is still poorly understood. In theory, ASB proliferation could have both catalytic and hampering effects on resident participation in community collective actions. On one hand, dissatisfaction with the quality of the living environment is conducive to more active involvement in housing governance (Yau, 2011a, 2013, 2014b). In this light, when the residents consider ASB a serious and intolerable problem in their neighborhoods, they should participate more active in housing governance to counter the delinquency and improve their living environment. On the other hand, proliferation of ASB or other neighborhood problems can weaken the social tie and bonding within a residential neighborhood (Oh, 2003). Besides, sense of powerlessness of the residents increases with stronger perceptions of ASB seriousness in a neighborhood (Geis and Ross, 1998). All these forces will in turn lead to the dwindled willingness of the residents to participate in community collective actions due to the weaker self and collective efficacy beliefs.

RESEARCH DESIGN

In view of the current research gaps, this study aims to explore the linkage between the levels of ASB proliferation and resident participation in MOH management. MOH management is a typical community collective action which is prone to the free-rider problem (Yau, 2013, 2014b). A structured questionnaire survey is conducted in Hong Kong to collect the information necessary for the empirical inquiries. Hong Kong is chosen as the research target because participation in the management affairs of MOH developments by individual residents in the city is virtually voluntary.

Analytic Model

To reveal the full picture of the relationships among level of ASB proliferation, perceived sense of community and participation behavior of residents, a path analytic approach is adopted in the current study. Figure 1 presents the posited model specifying the paths of influence of different variables on participation behavior. u and v are disturbances or residual terms which depict the effects of extraneous variables on perceived sense of community and participation level respectively.

Measures

As shown in the analytical model in Figure 1, the three key variables in this empirical study are a resident's participation level in housing management, level of ASB proliferation in his or her neighborhood and perceived sense of community. Making reference to previous studies on MOH management in Hong Kong like Yau (2013, 2014b), we measure the level of participation with the frequencies of four types of action in MOH management using a four-point scale (4 = very frequently or often; 3 = sometimes; 2 = seldom or rarely; 1 = never). These actions are a) attending resident association meetings; b) expressing views at resident association meetings; c) voting at resident association meetings; and d) organizing resident activities. The overall participation level of a resident is calculated as the arithmetic mean of the scores for the four aspects. A higher overall score means more active participation in housing management.

As for the level of ASB proliferation, it is ideal to employ objective or secondary data like number of ASB cases reported in the neighborhood where a resident lives in the past twelve months. However, this direction is impractical in many cases. Yau (2016) summarized the reasons for the impracticality and unreliability of using objective indicators to measure the extent or level of ASB proliferation. For example, the willingness of the victims of ASB incidents to report the cases to the public authorities is notoriously low (Casey and Flint, 2007, Bishop et al., 2009). Therefore, this study takes the level of ASB seriousness self-reported or perceived by an individual resident as a measure of the level of ASB proliferation. Although this measure is rather subjective, it may fit the current study best because it has been well believed that perception is a more important and direct factor to shape one's behavior. We measure the ASB perceptions by asking a resident to rate the level of seriousness of six broad types of ASB in his or her MOH development using a four-point scale (4 = very serious; 3 = serious; 2 = still tolerable; 1 = not an issue at all). The six types of ASB are a) noise nuisances; b) littering; c) uncontrolled animals; d) graffiti, fly-posting and vandalism; e) abusiveness of common areas; and f) intimidation and harassment. Again, the overall level of ASB seriousness perceived by a resident is calculated as the arithmetic mean of the scores for the six aspects. A higher overall score means a higher level of ASB seriousness perceived by the resident.

To gauge the sense of community perceived by a resident, a simplified version of the Sense of Community Index developed by Perkins et al. (1990) is adopted. The resident is asked about his or her views towards the following five statements using a four-point Likert scale (with 1 = strongly disagree; 2 = disagree; 3 = agree; and 4 = strongly agree):

1. My neighbours and I want the same things from the residential development.
2. I can recognize most of the residents in my residential development.
3. I feel at home in my residential development.
4. If there is a problem in my residential development, residents can get it solved.
5. Residents in my residential development generally get along well with each other.

An average score is calculated for a resident based on his or her answer to these four questions. A higher overall score means a higher level of sense of community perceived by the resident.

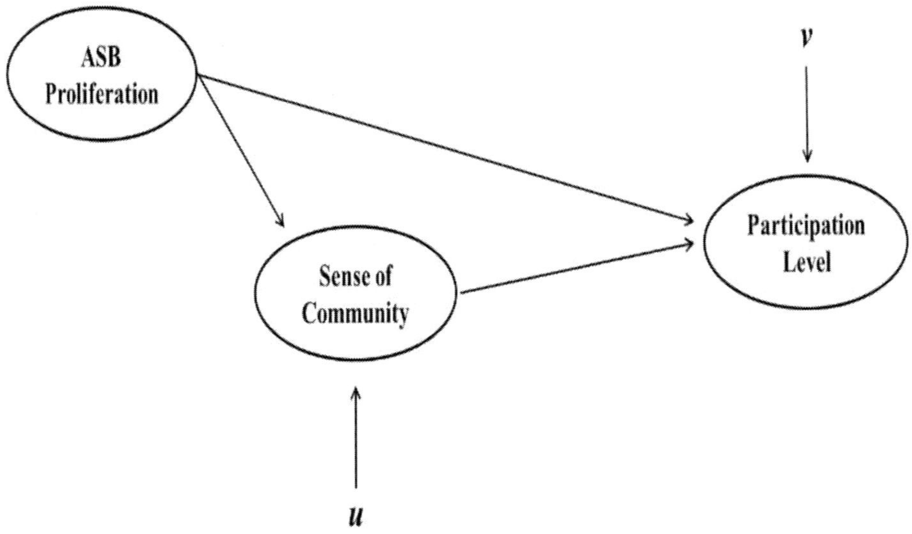

Figure 1. Posited model explaining resident participation in MOH management.

Participants

A self-administered online questionnaire survey was conducted in Hong Kong between April and May 2015. Six large-scale private multi-owned residential developments with at least 1,000 dwelling units in Hong Kong were randomly chosen as the study targets. These developments altogether had 10,731 units in total. 30% of the units in each chosen development were then randomly sampled. A letter was sent to each of the 3,221 units to invite the respective householders of the owner-occupied units to complete an anonymous online questionnaire. In the end, 617 questionnaires (19.2%) were returned. Among these returned questionnaires, 564 were complete and could be used for the analysis.

SURVEY FINDINGS AND ANALYSIS RESULTS

Table 1 summarizes the socio-demographic characteristics of the respondents. Eleven respondents (2.0%) were committee members of their resident associations. Cronbach's Alpha for the five-item sense of community scale is 0.901, implying a high degree of reliability of the scale. As shown in Table 2, noise is the most serious problem in the eyes of the respondents. On the contrary, intimidation and harassment is considered as the least serious problem. To facilitate the interpretation of the results, all non-dichotomous measures are linearly rescaled to the continuous [0, 1] range before model estimation. Table 3 summarizes the means and standard deviations for all measures after rescaling.

Correlation between ASB Proliferation and Sense of Community

The preliminary study by Yau (2014a) found a negative relationship between the levels of sense of community and ASB seriousness perceived by residents from Hong Kong's public and private housing sectors. In this regard, a negative correlation is assumed between the levels of ASB proliferation and sense of community perceived by the residents in this study. As expected, the calculation of the correlation coefficients shows the existence of a significant negative correlation between the two measures ($r = -0.31$; $p < 0.05$). In other words, when a resident perceives the ASB problem more serious in his or her neighborhood, he or she will have a weaker sense of community.

Table 1. Socio-demographic characteristics of the respondents (*n = 564*)

Characteristic		Proportion (%)
Gender	Male	74.65
	Female	25.35
Age	18-24 years old	4.79
	25-34 years old	12.06
	35-44 years old	27.66
	45-54 years old	37.41
	55-64 years old	16.31
	65 years old or above	1.77
Education level	Primary school or below	1.41
	Lower secondary school	6.03
	Upper secondary school or matriculation	22.34
	Sub-degree post-secondary education	17.91
	Bachelor degree	44.15
	Postgraduate degree	8.16
Personal monthly income	HK$9,999 or below	3.36
	HK$10,000-19,999	14.72
	HK$20,000-29,999	17.20
	HK$30,000-39,999	35.11
	HK$40,000-49,999	22.16
	HK$50,000 or above	7.45

Table 2. Self-reported levels of ASB proliferation by type

Type of ASB	Mean	Standard Deviation
Noise nuisances	2.91	1.10
Littering	2.85	1.13
Uncontrolled animals	2.38	1.14
Graffiti, fly-posting and vandalism	2.38	1.12
Abusiveness of common areas	2.39	1.08
Intimidation and harassment	2.32	1.11

Table 3. Descriptive statistics of all measures after rescaling

Variable	Mean	Standard Deviation
ASB proliferation	0.52	0.25
Participation level	0.51	0.17
Sense of community	0.58	0.22

Correlation between ASB Proliferation and Participation Level

As revealed by Yau (2013, 2014b), residents are more willing to participate in MOH governance if they nurse a grievance against the poor housing management outcomes such as unclean or unhygienic conditions and threats of crime. Therefore, a positive correlation between ASB perceptions and participation level is envisaged. Nonetheless, there is no observed correlation between the two measures ($r = 0.05$; $p > 0.1$). That means there is no direct association between levels of ASB proliferation and resident participation in housing management affairs.

Correlation between Sense of Community and Participation Level

To a very large extent, governance or management of a MOH development necessitates collective actions of the residents, particularly the homeowners. While a external property management agent can be appointed to help the residents take care of the daily routines of housing management, resident participation is still essential. On account of the collective-good nature of the housing management outcomes (e.g., cleaner places and safer environment), however, collective actions in MOH management are very often prone to the free-rider problem (Yau, 2013). Bengtsson (1998, 2000) suggested that participation of residents could be promoted by strengthening the social ties or sense of community among the residents so they would have higher levels of mutual trust and reciprocity. Empirical studies like Yau (2013, 2014b) also evidenced that the level of sense of community perceived by a MOH resident was positively associated with his or her participation level in housing management affairs. Thus, in the current study, a positive relationship between the levels of sense of community and resident participation is expected. We find a positive correlation between the two measures ($r = 0.32$; $p < 0.01$).

Path Analysis

To test the structural model in Figure 1 which combines levels of ASB proliferation, sense of community and participation in MOH management, we conducted a path analysis on the survey data using the software SPSS AMOS

22.0. Following many previous studies like Maruyama and McGarvey (1980), Schumacker and Lomax (1996) and Hodges et al. (2013), the suitability of the model for the data in the current research is evaluated using the maximum likelihood estimation technique. With this approach, we can say that the data fit the estimated model well if the normal fit index (NFI) and comparative fit index (CFI) are both greater than 0.9 while the root-mean-square error of approximation (RMSEA) is less than 0.05.

The results of the path analysis testing for the hypothesized relationships are shown in Figure 2. The diagram shows the verified model with standardized path coefficients which are found statistically significant at the 10% level at least. For the estimated model, the NFI, CFI and RMSEA value 0.937, 0.951 and 0.049 respectively, implying a very good fit of the model to the data. Only two path coefficients are statistically significant at the 10% level at least. Similar to the results of correlation tests aforementioned, the effect of ASB proliferation on sense of community is negative ($\beta = -0.31$; $p < 0.05$) and that of sense of community on participation level ($\beta = 0.32$; $p < 0.01$). On the other hand, the path coefficient for the path 'ASB Proliferation → Participation Level' is not significant even at the 10% level.

DISCUSSION

The objective of this research, we should recall, is to explore the structural relationships between ASB proliferation in a neighborhood and participation level of residents in housing management affairs. The analytic model in Figure 1 attempts to differentiate direct and indirect effects of ASB proliferation on participation level. The verified model in Figure 2 suggests that sense of community perceived by a resident is directly dependent on ASB proliferation which is measured with the seriousness of ASB problem in his or her residential neighborhoods perceived by the same resident. Perceived sense of community in turn has a positive impact on the resident's level of participation in housing management affairs. The results show that direct significant effect of ASB proliferation on participation level is absent.

In keeping with the previous empirical findings, this study find a negative correlation between ASB proliferation and sense of community and a positive association between sense of community and participation level. By combining the two paths, we can infer a negative, though indirect, relationship between ASB proliferation and participation level. These findings enrich our knowledge about the impacts of ASB proliferation on a residential neighborhood – a serious problem of ASB diminishes a neighborhood's capacity to building up an effective management system by discouraging residents to participate. To put it another way, in order to promote a culture of active resident participation in housing management, stakeholders (e.g., governments, resident associations and locally-based concern groups) need to lower the perceived levels of ASB proliferation in residential neighborhoods. This goal is can be achieved by various means. For example, the problem of ASB proliferation can be curbed with stricter social control (e.g., stepped-up enforcements of deed of mutual covenant and heavier sanctions against perpetrators). Besides, programs can be designed to help residents understand and respect different life styles within a residential community.

In addition, the analysis results also suggest that resident participation can be promoted through strengthening the sense of community among the residents. In this sense, the multi-pronged approach to community building proposed by Yau (2010) is applicable. Passive measures like adopting more open housing design to facilitate social interactions among residents and active measures like organizing activities to let residents know each other better are plausibly effective in building up sense of community among the residents and in turn harnessing residents' willingness to participate in housing management affairs.

Apart from the practical insights discussed above, the research findings also have significant academic value. They add to Shaw and McKay's (1969) social disorganization theory which posits that delinquencies are more likely to happen in disadvantaged neighborhoods or disorganized communities. The analysis results of this study evidence that social disorganization (e.g., weak social bonds) is conducive to neighborhood disorder. In other words, the relationship between social disorganization and delinquency should be bi-directional rather than unidirectional.

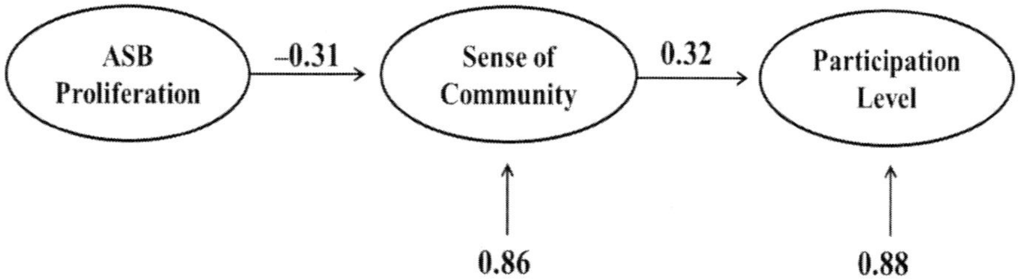

Figure 2. Verified model with standardized path coefficients.

The originality of the tested model consisted in considering the effect of ASB perceptions on the levels of sense of community and participation in housing management simultaneously by assigning the status of mediator variable to sense of community. Nonetheless, the current research is not free of limitations. First, the respondents come from six large-scale private MOH developments in Hong Kong only. The variation in the ASB seriousness perceived by the residents from these six developments may not be large enough for more insightful analysis. The variation or differentiation can be augmented if more housing developments of different scales and classes are covered. Moreover, some other factors which may have significant impacts on participation level are not included in the analytic model of this study. These factors include perceptional variables like self efficacy belief and contextual variables such as presence of resident association and development scale.

Conclusion and Agenda for Further Research

For better well-being of the local communities, ASB in residential neighborhoods should not be overlooked. Yet, empirical study on the impacts of ASB proliferation is lacking in the East. In particular, how ASB affects community collective actions like partaking in housing management affairs has not been investigated. The question of the link between residents' ASB perceptions and participation level in housing management is the subject of this research. Drawing on the findings of a structured questionnaire survey on private MOH residents in Hong Kong, this research has clarified some aspects about the relation between ASB perceptions and participation level of the residents. The results show that when an individual resident perceives the problem of ASB as more serious in his or her residential neighborhood, he or she will participate less actively in housing management affairs. The negative association is moderated by the sense of community perceived by the resident. With a view to the research findings, to promote resident participation in housing management affairs in the city, the local government may need to take various initiatives like stricter control of ASB in housing communities and fostering sense of community among residents. It is hoped that the insights of this study will help identify drivers which can further motivate residents in Hong Kong to contribute to the effective management of their housing.

This chapter tries to extend the knowledge frontier to an area that has been largely ignored before – the effects of perceived ASB seriousness in a living environment on an individual's participation in community collective actions.

It establishes a new link between the social disorganization theory and ASB and promotes more scholarly inquiries into this research area. For instance, the current study is a cross-sectional one. Further studies should be warranted to test the structural relationship between ASB proliferation and resident participation in housing management longitudinally. Moreover, more contextual factors such as property management regime and design of MOH development can be taken into account in future research. Furthermore, cross-cultural comparative studies can be conducted so that whether the findings of this study can be generalized to other cities can be verified.

ACKNOWLEDGMENTS

The work described in this chapter was supported jointly by a grant from the Research Grants Council of the Hong Kong Special Administrative Region, China [Project No. CityU 11410214] and the Research Grant Writing Fund of the College of Liberal Arts and Social Sciences, City University of Hong Kong.

REFERENCES

Agyemang, C., Van Hooijdonk, C., Wendel-Vos, W., Lindeman, E., Stronks, K. and Droomers, M. (2007). The association of neighbourhood psychosocial stressors and self-rated health in Amsterdam, the Netherlands. *Journal of epidemiol community health*, 61, 1042-1049.

Andersen, H. S. (2008). Why do residents want to leave deprived neighbourhoods? The importance of residents' subjective evaluations of their neighbourhood and its reputation. *Journal of housing and the built environment*, 23, 79-101.

Australian Bureau of Statistics. (2006). *Crime and safety, Australia (April 2005)*. Sydney: Australian Bureau of Statistics.

Bengtsson, B. (1998). Tenants' dilemma: On collection action in housing. *Housing Studies*, 13, 99-120.

Bengtsson, B. (2000). Solving the tenants' dilemma: Collective action and norms of co-operation in housing. *Housing, Theory and Society*, 17, 175-187.

Bishop, V., Cassel, C.M. and Hiel, H. (2009). Preserving masculinity in service work: An exploration of the underreporting of customer anti-social behaviour. *Human relations*, 62, 5-25.

Brown, A. (2004). Anti-social behaviour, crime control and social control. *The Howard Journal of criminal justice*, 43, 203-211.

Brown, J. (2011). *A municipal exigency: An exploration of the correlation of physical and social incivilities on the decline of residential property values in Richmond, VA*. Richmond: Virginia Commonwealth University.

Cale, E. M. (2006). A quantitative review of the relations between the 'Big 3' higher order personality dimensions and antisocial behaviour. *Journal of research in personality*, 40, 250-284.

Casey, R. and Flint, J. (2007). Active citizenship in the governance of anti-social behaviour in the UK: Exploring the non-reporting of incidents. *People, place and policy*, 1/2, 69-79.

Chartered Institute of Housing. (1995). *Neighbour nuisance: Ending the nightmare*. Coventry: The Chartered Institute of Housing.

Chartered Institute of Housing. (2001). *The law: An adequate response to anti-social behaviour*. Cardiff: Chartered Institute of Housing.

Curtis, L. J., Dooley, M. D. and Phipps, S. A. (2004). Child well-being and neighbourhood quality: Evidence from the Canadian national longitudinal survey of children and youth. *Social science and medicine*, 58, 1917-1927.

Deery, M. and Jago, D. (2010). Social impacts of evens and the role of anti-social behavior. *International journal of even and festival management*, 1, 8-28.

Department for Communities and Local Government. (2011). *A new mandatory power of possession for anti-social behaviour: Consultation.* London: Department for Communities and Local Government.

Dunn, J. R. (2000). Housing and health inequalities: review and prospects for research. *Housing studies*, 15, 341-366.

Eysenck, H. J. (1996) Personality and crime: where do we stand. *Psychology, Crime and Law*, 2, 143-152.

Geis, K.J. and Ross, C.E. (1998). A new look at urban alienation: The effect of neighborhood disorder on perceived powerlessness. *Social psychology quarterly*, 61, 232-246.

Glasgow Housing Association. (2007). *Tackling antisocial behaviour in Glasgow: An evaluation of policy and practice in Glasgow Housing Association*. Glasgow: Glasgow Housing Association.

Hodges, M., Godbout, N., Briere, J., Lanktree, C., Gilbert, A. and Kletzka, N.T. (2013). Cumulative trauma and symptom complexity in children: A path analysis. *Child Abuse and Neglect*, 37, 891-898.

Home Office. (2003). *Respect and responsibility: Taking a stand against anti-social behaviour*. London: Home Office.

Hope, T. and Hough, M. (1988). Area, crime and incivilities: A profile from the British crime survey. In: T. Hope (Ed.), *Communities and crime reduction* (pp. 30-44). London: HMSO.

Housing and Development Board. (2010). *Public housing in Singapore: Well-being of communities, families and the elderly: HDB sample household survey 2008*. Singapore: Housing and Development Board.

Hunter, C., Nixon, J. and Slatter, M. (2005). Neighbours behaving badly: anti-social behaviour, property rights and exclusion in England and Australia. *Macquarie law journal*, 5, 149-176.

Innes, M. (1999). An iron fist in an iron glove? The zero-tolerance policing debate. *Howard journal of criminal justice*, 38, 397-410.

Innes, M. and Weston, N. (2010). *Re-thinking the policing of anti-social behaviour*. London: HMIC.

Ipsos MORI. (2006). *Public attitudes to parenting*, available at website: http://www.ipsos-mori.com/researchpublications/researcharchive/poll.aspx?oItemId=374 [accessed on January 23 2016].

Ipsos MORI. (2010). *Policing anti-social behaviour: The public perspective*. London: Ipsos MORI.

Jacobs, K. and Arthurson, K. (2003). *Development effective housing management policies to address problems of anti-social behaviour*. Melbourne: Australian Housing and Urban Research Institute.

Jacobson, J., Millie, A. and Hough, M. (2008). Why tackle anti-social behaviour. In: P. Squires (Ed.), *ASBO nation: The criminalisation of nuisance* (pp. 37-55). Bristol: Policy Press.

Kerig, P.K. and Becker, S.P. (2015). Early abuse and neglect as risk factors for the development of criminal and antisocial behavior. In: J. Morizot and L. Kazemian (Eds.), *The Development of criminal and antisocial behavior: Theory, research and practical applications* (pp. 181-199). Cham: Springer.

LaGrange, R.L., Ferraro, K.F. and Supancic, M. (1992). Perceived risk and fear of crime: Role of social and physical incivilities. *Journal of research in crime and delinquency*, 9, 311-334.

Latkin, C.A. and Curry, A.D. (2003). Stressful neighborhoods and depression: A prospective study of the impact of neighborhood disorder. *Journal of health and social behavior*, 44, 34-44.

Latkin, C.A., Williams, C.T., Wang, J. and Curry, A.D. (2005). Neighborhood social disorder as a determinant of drug injection behaviors: A structural equation modeling approach. *Health psychology*, 24, 96-100.

Mackenzie, S., Bannister, J., Flint, J., Parr, S., Millie, A. and Fleetwood, J. (2010). *The drivers of perceptions of anti-social behaviour (Research report no. 34)*. London: Home Office.

Maruyama, G. and McGravey, B. (1980). Evaluating causal models: An application of maximum-likelihood analysis of structural equations. *Psychological bulletin*, 87, 502-512.

Millie, A. (2009). *Anti-social behaviour*. Berkshire: Open University Press.

Millie, A., Jacobson, J., McDonald, E. and Hough, M. (2005). *Anti-social behaviour strategies: Finding a balance*. Bristol, Policy Press.

Morizot, J. (2015). The contribution of temperament and personality traits to criminal and antisocial behavior development and desistance. In: J. Morizot and L. Kazemian (Eds.), *The Development of criminal and antisocial behavior: Theory, research and practical applications* (pp. 137-165). Cham: Springer.

Newcombe, R. G., Lyons, R. A., Jones, S. J. and Patterson, J. (2005). Home injuries and built form: methodological issues and developments in database link. *BioMed central health services research*, 5, 1-6.

Nixon, J., Blandy, S., Hunter, C., Jones, A. and Reeve, K. (2003). *Developing good practice in tackling anti-social behaviour in mixed tenure areas*. Sheffield: Sheffield Hallam University.

Oh, J. (2003). Assessing the social bonds of elderly neighbors: The roles of length of residence, crime victimization, and perceived disorder. *Sociological inquiry*, 73, 490-510.

Perkins, D.D. and Taylor, R.B. (1996). Ecological assessments of community disorder: Their relationship to fear of crime and theoretical implications. *American journal of community psychology*, 24, 63-107.

Raw, G. J. and Hamilton, R. M. (1995). *Building regulation and health*. Garston: Building Research Establishment.

Schumacker, R.E. and Lomax, R.G. (1996). *A beginner's guide to structural equation modeling*. Mahwah: Lawrence Erlbaum.

Shaw, C.R. and McKay, H.D. (1969). *Juvenile delinquency and urban areas*. Chicago: The University of Chicago Press.

South Kesteven District Council. (2016). *Anti-social behaviour*, available at website http://www.southkesteven.gov.uk/index.aspx?articleid=8355 [access on May 28, 2016].

United States Census Bureau. (2010). *American housing survey for the United States: 2009 – Current housing report.* Washington DC: United States Department of Housing and Urban Development and United States Census Bureau.

Upson, A. (2006). *Perceptions and experience of anti-social behaviour: Findings from the 2004/05 British crime survey*. London: Home Office.

Wilson, J.Q. and Kelling, G. (1982). Broken windows: The police and neighborhood safety. *The Altantic Monthly*, March 1982.

Wong, S.K., Cheung, A.K.C., Yau, Y., Ho, D.C.W. and Chau, K.W. (2006). Are our residential buildings healthy and safe? A survey in Hong Kong. *Structural survey*, 24, 77-86.

Wood, M. (2004). *Perceptions and experience of anti-social behaviour: Findings from 2003/2004 British crime survey*. London: Home Office.

Yau, Y. (2010). Sense of community and homeowner participation in housing management: A study of Hong Kong. *Urbani izziv*, 21, 126-135.

Yau, Y. (2011a). Collectivism and activism in housing management in Hong Kong. *Habitat international*, 35, 327-334.

Yau, Y. (2011b). On the anti-social behaviour control in Hong Kong's public housing. *Housing studies*, 26, 701-722.

Yau, Y. (2012). Insignificant or ignored? Antisocial behaviour in private housing in Hong Kong. *Urbani izziv*, 23, 103-111.

Yau, Y. (2013). Willingness to participate in collective action: The case of multiowned housing management, *Journal of urban affairs*, 35, 153-171.

Yau, Y. (2014a). Anti-social behaviour management: A communitarian approach. *Habitat international*, 42, 245-252.

Yau, Y. (2014b). Perceived efficacies and collectivism in multi-owned housing management. *Habitat international*, 43, 133-141.

Yau, Y. (2016). Benchmarking the extent of quality-of-life crime: A study in Hong Kong's public housing sector. In: A. Klein (ed.) *Crime and criminal behavior*. New York: Nova Science, forthcoming.

In: Antisocial Behavior ISBN: 978-1-53612-954-0
Editors: Abby Dobson and Peter Talbot © 2017 Nova Science Publishers, Inc.

Chapter 3

Dating Violence in First Romantic Relationships

Estefanía Estévez[1] and Amapola Povedano[2]
[1]Universidad Miguel Hernández de Elche, Alicante, Spain
[2]Universidad Pablo de Olavide de Sevilla, Spain
Quizá una tercera persona

Abstract

This short communication focuses on violent behavior perpetrated in adolescents' first romantic relationships, a fact that can establish behavioral patterns for future relations in adulthood. The first section of this chapter includes the definition of dating violence and the different types of gender violence, as well as the mechanisms operating in situations of intimate partner violence during adolescence. Following this, the main causes of violence, grounded in the Ecological Systems Theory of Human Development, are outlined. Finally, the consequences of such behavior for victims are analyzed. The chapter ends with a summary of the main ideas and provides some final recommendations for prevention.

What is Dating Gender Violence?

We can define gender violence in a couple as the repeated abusive behavior of a man against a woman he maintains or has maintained a sentimental relationship with, where his purpose is to exert his control and dominance over the woman and the relationship (Povedano, 2014). To achieve his goal, an abusive man can use subtle measures like isolation, control, devaluation or other more evident measures like shouting, insults, humiliations, accusations, threats, emotional abuse, sexual abuse or any other effective strategies involving violence to achieve his purpose. This is not domestic violence but violence that "domesticates" (Povedano, Jiménez & Valdivieso, 2013).

The first romantic relationships are normally formed during adolescence and can set the pattern for girls' and boys' behaviors in future relationships (Billingham, Bland & Leary, 1999; Lewis & Fremouw, 2001). These first relationships can range from occasional and chance encounters involving the exploratory behaviors typical of intimate and sexual adolescent encounters that parents or teachers are not aware of, to deeper relationships where the ties are stronger and which reference adults are usually informed about. In both cases, situations of gender violence with clearly defined mechanisms can occur in a couple: the cycle of violence and the process of violence (Povedano, 2014).

An aggressor's main purpose is to dominate his victim. Therefore, when physical violence appears, the abuser has normally already established a previous pattern of verbal, psychological, financial or sexual abuse. Physical violence is "only" used if other forms of violence are not effective. Although there are different typologies of gender violence (Foshee, Bauman, Linder, Rice & Wilcher, 2007), Table 1 shows one of the classifications which in the authors' opinion includes types of gender violence according to its characteristics.

Table 1. Types of gender violence

- *Physical:* behaviors that go from a slap to more extreme cases like murder. Besides putting health at risk and in the most extreme cases the lives of the people assaulted, physical abuse also causes intense fear and feelings of humiliation.
- *Psychological*: behaviors that include verbal and emotional aspects. Here, the actions included are, for example, insults, contempt and humiliations. It also involves behaviors like ignoring (not speaking to someone or making them feel they do not exist), blackmail and also threats.
- *Sexual*: implies any unwanted sexual contact. From groping to rape.
- *Financial*: refers to behavior that involves the financial control of the victim. It includes acts like forbidding or stopping women from achieving their own sources of income to the point of not providing financial resources for basic housekeeping expenses.

Particularly in adolescent boys, romantic relations marked by physical violence can include pushing, hitting, kicking, slapping, pinching, hair pulling, strangling or punching. Psychological violence includes behaviors like insults or calling girls by nasty nicknames, frequently being jealous, threatening to harm them or to commit suicide if they do not do what they want, not letting the girls go out with their friends, trying to locate them constantly (for example, on their mobiles) or dictating what clothes they should wear. Sexual abuse includes behaviors like groping and unwanted kisses, forced sexual relations, forbidding the use of contraceptives or girls being forced into sexual games. Finally, financial abuse can include behaviors of controlling spending (for example on clothes or make-up), or to encourage a woman to leave her job which provides her with income and independence (Capaldi, Dishion, Stoolmiller & Yoerger, 2001).

Physical abuse usually represents the visible part of an iceberg, the larger part of which is not so evident and is translated into numerous subtle types of violence tolerated by girls and which they adapt to over time (Díaz-Aguado & Carvajal, 2010). In fact, gender violence in a couple is a type of violence with some distinctive characteristics compared to other types of violence, so we cannot expect victims of gender violence to behave like other victims. For example, many victims get to the point of not responding to the aggressions because they remain blocked or paralyzed (Povedano, 2014). In psychology, this type of behavior is called *learned helplessness*, that is to say, when any response by the victim is punished by the aggressor, there comes a time when a woman is unable to produce any response, which completely undermines her possibilities of escaping or fleeing from the situation.

The Cycle of Gender Violence

Women who regularly suffer gender violence are not constantly assaulted. Normally, the relationship alternates periods of tension and violence with other periods of calm and even affection. This alternation actually becomes a cycle of gender violence, which generates a high mutual dependence and consists of three clearly different phases; tension building, violent outburst and honeymoon (Walker, 1977).

The first phase of *tension building* is characterized by unexpected mood swings, anger about unimportant issues and irritability in men. In this first phase, women tend to avoid conflict at all cost, modifying their behavior so that their partner does not get angry or upset, trying to be condescending and anticipating their whims to please them. Women usually justify their partners' behaviors to their relations and friends, making excuses for them and hoping that it is just a rough patch which will soon pass. Normally, tension continues to build up and upsets tend to last longer, accompanied by small fights, arguments and shouting until an external event triggers the next phase.

The second phase, *violent outburst*, involves a release of the tension that has built up in the previous phase and consists of an acute violent episode. Abusers can use any type of violence (physical, psychological, sexual or financial) to punish those behaviors by women that they do not see as appropriate. An abuser's main purpose is to both harm and dominate his victim. In this way, the acute incident ends when the abuser considers the victim has "learnt her lesson". His way of causing harm evolves over time towards less visible and evident ways, so as not leave demonstrable traces. This fact indicates that they have control over their violent behavior, since they selectively unleash their violence against women.

The abuser usually blames the woman for the appearance of this second phase, using the upsets that she has caused him during the phase of tension building to justify his behavior and, on occasions, he will attribute it to drink or other external stress factors. After this phase of unleashing violence is over, the victim is left in a state of shock, not wanting to believe what has happened to her, minimizing the attack suffered and the injuries received and even denying the situation that has just taken place (Janoff-Bulman & Frieze, 1983).

In the final phase, called *honeymoon* or repentance, the tension and violence decrease until they disappear. The aggressor usually recognizes he is to blame and asks for forgiveness, promising there will be changes; for example, he will not engage in violent behaviors again, or even that he will start psychological treatment. He tries to manipulate the victim, arguing that if she does not forgive him it will destroy his life, the family's life or that it is going to hurt their sons and daughters or friends (Hunnicutt, 2009). The aggressor expresses how he needs her to help him and usually makes threats of suicide if his wife leaves him. In this phase, the man is once again attentive, affectionate, friendly and respectful towards the woman, because he is afraid that after the violent attack she will end the relationship. In fact, some women who have suffered gender violence recognize that their authentic honeymoon happened after the first acute violent attack and not during the period immediately after their marriage.

Victimization of women deepens as the relationship of dependence between victim and aggressor becomes more consolidated (women think men are not monsters because on occasions they can be marvelous). In this phase, a woman who has made the decision to end the relationship will give up this idea in the face of a man's emotional and affective manipulation. In fact, in the event that previous charges have been made against their aggressor, many women usually withdraw them, and their hope that everything in the relationship will change becomes real. However, most of the time, nothing changes and the cycle begins again with the building up of tension, as represented graphically in the figure below. (1479)

Furthermore, the cycle is a spiral that changes shape and increases in intensity every time it is repeated. Consequently, the time it takes to complete the cycle is shortened: the tension building phase is completed more quickly, in the violent outburst phase the intensity of violence increases, and the repentance or honeymoon phase tends to disappear. When the cycle of violence is established in a couple's relationship, it is very difficult to stop it. For this reason, it is fundamental for us to be aware of the process of gender violence in order to detect and prevent adolescent couples falling into this growing spiral.

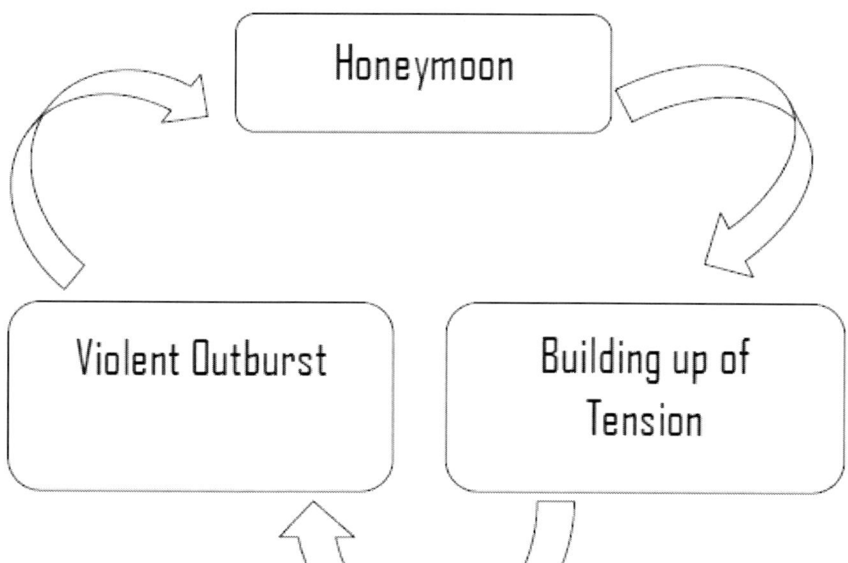

Figure 1. Cycle of gender violence.

THE PROCESS OF GENDER VIOLENCE

Gender violence in a couple appears in the first romantic relations, which are usually initiated during adolescence. Violent behaviors can initially occur unnoticed as they are subtle acts that favor inequality between sexes and lead women towards subservience (Hunnicutt, 2009). In the beginning, the abuser creates the conditions necessary to be able to dominate and control the victim with the purpose that it should be the women herself, who through manipulation, falls deeper into the process of violence. The first step of the process of gender violence is the creation and consolidation of a system of dominance over the woman based on three basic tools: isolation, control and devaluation.

Isolation. The abuser will try to isolate the victim from her network of family relations and friendships by all means available to him, since this first step is fundamental for him to able to use the other tools of dominance (Lila, Gracia, & Murgui, 2013). The majority of abusers usually use very subtle techniques that involve behaviors that favor the woman distancing herself from her relationships or their deterioration over time. However, others opt for more evident and coercive means like directly forbidding relationships or through confinement.

Jealousy, as we will see in the following section, is one of the myths of romantic love and for the majority of women, and especially for adolescents, it is an unmistakable expression of love. However, the aggressor usually uses jealousy to isolate the victim from all the people who surround her like friends, relations, neighbors and school friends or colleagues. Although he does not directly forbid her from these things, the abuser's aim is for the woman not to relate to other people and for her contacts even by telephone to disappear.

The aggressor usually creates uncomfortable situations and behaves humiliatingly, violently or embarrassingly before friends and family relations who, on many occasions and without realizing it, become involuntary accomplices by avoiding inviting the couple to social and cultural gatherings or paying them visits. On other occasions, the victim voluntarily distances herself from her network of social support, with some perverse consequences: loss of contacts, models, help, and more importantly, loss of objective points of view about aspects of her relationship which are clear signs of being in danger of gender violence.

Control. Control is initiated over aspects that could appear to be unimportant, like, for example, clothes or make-up. However, control over more important aspects in life like relationships, timetables, activities etc. will be established gradually and progressively. Initially, the aggressor will use subtle behaviors, like getting angry or not speaking until he reaches the point of more categorical and direct acts like insults and punishments (Herrera, Expósito, & Moya, 2012). The victim usually gives in on aspects that seem less important, trying to avoid conflicts with her partner at all costs. This generates such serious negative consequences for her that she voluntarily and progressively stops using the conflict management and negotiation tools fundamental to establishing a healthy relationship between a couple, like, for example, defending her opinion about a specific issue that is important to her.

Another of the aspects the abuser tries to dominate the victim with is financial control. This control is not only exerted on women who are financially dependent (for example, giving the victim little money for the housekeeping which forces her to continually beg him for money), but also on women with financial independence (for example, making important financial decisions without consulting her. This control can turn into situations of financial violence when, for example, the aggressor applies for credit or gets into debt or family assets, which she is also responsible for, are sold without her agreement.

Devaluation. The use of this tool by the aggressor brings to the fore the patriarchal belief that men are superior to women. They are behaviors which systematically try to take away the value of a woman's abilities, opinions, emotions and actions. Victims will suffer constant devaluation, leading to serious consequences for them such as loss of self-esteem, which is one of the fundamental sources for a balanced development. In addition, we cannot forget that the victims have already been isolated from other relationships, so they have lost other sources of self-esteem which could counterbalance systematic devaluation by the abuser.

The process is completed when the system of domination is consolidated, that is to say, when the aggressor regularly uses the tools of isolation, control and devaluation. He may use them in parallel or he may try out different tactics until he identifies the ones that function better (for example, insulting the woman in front of her parents includes devaluation, but it is also a subtle form of isolation).

Normally, victims do not believe that these acts can be considered as gender violence, and consequently that they can be reported to the authorities. If we want to understand why victims of gender violence do not report it, or if they do report it, why they withdraw the charges on several occasions and tolerate situations that can be compared to the most perverse torture (Gracia, E. & Herrero, 2006), it is fundamental to understand how the cycle of violence and the consolidation process of the domination system function as the invisible foundations of gender violence in a couple.

CAUSES ASSOCIATED TO GENDER VIOLENCE IN ADOLESCENCE: ECOLOGICAL MODEL AND THE CONTEXTS OF INFLUENCE

In the ecological model of human development (Bronfenbrenner, 1979), human beings are considered to be integrated in a dense network of relations which represent the most significant development contexts or environments. In this sense, behavior is understood to be the result of the interaction between a person and different systems that superimpose one another and relate bi-directionally. If we analyze the problem of teen dating violence (TDV) from this perspective, we must consider that its causes are numerous and complex and it is necessary to examine them in terms of interaction between people and contexts. In keeping with this idea, it is essential to analyze the main contextual factors (family, school, community and the media) associated to TDV problems (Heise, 1998; Povedano, Monreal & Ferrer, 2014).

General Contextual Factors

The myths and beliefs about romantic love are deeply rooted cognitive structures which to a great extent determine the ideas about romantic relationships adolescents consider as "normal" (Cleveland, Herrera & Stuewig, 2003). All of them are deeply rooted in a cultural model based on the inequality and imbalance in the relations between men and women, a model which is transmitted from one generation to the next through gender socialization. The socialization process is the transmission of values, beliefs, standards, attitudes and ways of behaving appropriate to the society an individual belongs to, so that the socialized person assumes socially valued objectives as the principles-guide to their behavior,

Gender socialization refers specifically to the process whereby people come to think and act differently according to whether they are men or women; each woman and each man is formed through models, through socially shared images which each person identifies with. Each man and each woman are expected to assume a "suitably" assigned gender role (Povedano,

2013). If being integrated in a culture means assuming the roles that define it, when these roles are not met, this means breaking, confronting, or changing deeply-rooted rules with the consequent emotional loss that this involves.

Violence is also socialized and it is learnt. In this context, some authors have identified that the greater involvement of boys in types of physical aggression could be due to learning from "patterns of violence that are differentiated according to gender" (Estévez, Povedano, Jiménez & Musitu, 2012; White, 2002). The socialization process, whereby some people assume rules and behavior standards, fundamentally takes place in the context of the family. However, we should consider that during adolescence there are other microsystems or immediate contexts of development which are as or more important than the family for young people, such as peers or school. Added to these socializing agents, there is now the mass media, which is found in the micro-social environment, which transmits many of the myths, beliefs and representations of love and violence.

Peers

The relationship with peers plays a fundamental role in the development of TDV. It has specifically been determined that being involved with groups of violent friends at school increases the risk of adolescents exerting violence in their romantic relationships (Capaldi & cols., 2001). Maintaining close ties with a violent peer group at school can lead to a certain social contagion of negative attitudes towards relationships between men and women, reinforcing beliefs and attitudes that justify aggressions as acceptable and normal in affective dating relationships. In fact, during adolescence, violent behavior can be a habitual way of relating with peers, and this tendency in adolescents' behavior can influence affective relationships and dating relationships which are formed during this stage (Muñoz-Rivas, Grana, O'Leary & González, 2007). As mentioned before, having close contact with an adolescent aggressor seems to be the strongest predictor of violence in a future relationship (Vézina & Hérbert, 2007).

Furthermore, research has also shown that adolescents who are victims of school violence have a high risk of suffering TDV (Arriaga & Foshee, 2004; Vézina & Hérbert, 2007), thereby broadening victimization and its consequences to different spheres of adolescent life. We consider that this confluence of abuse in different relationships that are important to victimized adolescents builds up a situation of serious risk that can lead to low self-esteem and strong devaluation, a deep dissatisfaction with their own life and possible suicidal ideation. Therefore, it is necessary to provide steps for detecting these situations and to pay special attention to monitoring these cases through all the socializing agents, and especially in the educational environment.

The Family

The family is perhaps one of the areas that has been most researched in the attempt to explain TDV (Barnett, Miller-Perrin & Perrin, 1997). The intimate relationship that a father and mother have is the first romantic relationship that children are witness to. For example, in their research, Foshee and colleagues (2005) found there was a relationship between TDV and having witnessed or having been the target of violence in the family of origin, independently of gender, and mediated through the acceptance of this violence and an aggressive style of solving conflicts.

According to Vézina and Hérbert (2007) in a review of articles published from 1986 to 2006, the main family risk factors related to TDV are: punitive parenting practices, lack of affective bonding, frequent conflicts, inadequate family communication patterns, violent marital relations and physical and sexual abuse of children by parents.

Therefore, the value of these initial learning experiences through observation is of absolute importance. Sometimes adolescents from cold and distant family homes are observed to become involved in overwhelming romantic (controlling, jealous, intense) relationships as a kind of "compensatory action". However, a parenting style that establishes clear limits for youngsters, combined with relations between parents marked by an affective intimacy and open and positive communication seems to protect adolescents from TDV (Vézina & Hérbert, 2007).

School: Adolescents' Relationship with Teachers

In the school context, it is important to highlight that it is only recently that gender socialization and the need to include it among educational objectives is now being contemplated. The first step towards this is the inclusion of related transversal areas in the school curriculum. The school itself has become an ideal place for carrying out a critical analysis of the everyday reality of adolescents because of its characteristics of coexistence and education, as well as the non-formal educational messages through the media or peers. The aim of this type of education should be to transform the social and cultural bases which currently generate discrimination between sexes (Povedano, Muñiz, Cuesta & Musitu, 2015). In this context, within the national plans of eradication of violence against women, interventions have been designed to prevent gender violence and foster behaviors of equality in schools (see review, Cornelius & Resseguie, 2007).

As in the case of parents, teachers are significant and close to adolescents, and ultimately they are important models of behavior in inter-gender relations and solving conflicts. For example, teachers should take special care not to reward those violent practices that are socially associated to masculinity. Teachers have access to tools like education in equality or co-education and the development of classroom activities which allow youngsters to identify and question the myths and beliefs that sustain TDV.

The Media

The media has become an essential characteristic of the contemporary world, and in a globalized world it is immediate and easily accessible. In contrast to other periods of history, contemporary couples are no longer limited to being formed by just being exposed to the model of close family and the community, but they are now formed under the important models presented through the media. Therefore, through television, the internet and video games, today's adolescents find an important and fundamental source of models on which to build a social representation of love that guides their romantic behavior.

To be exact, television series seem to be a particularly important genre for adolescents, and many of them are designed especially for this audience. Television series are considered an ideal genre for studying the transmission of values because they represent stories close to everyday life and construct models which provide a variety of characters that can function as examples. These programs reflect issues that are highly relevant to the stage of life adolescents are going through (friendship, romances, relationships with parents), and they can evaluate their own personal situation and learn from the reference they have before their eyes to solve conflicts or to deal with different situations.

Therefore, the media is not neutral but transmits ideas about standards, structure and social behavior (Theory of cultivation: Gerbner, Gross, Morgan & Signorielli, 1994). However, other factors, and importantly parenting interactions and styles, intervene in this process in such a way that each adolescent perceives television content with "their own glasses". However, although television preferences come from personal choices, they do reflect family values and attitudes. Therefore, on the one hand, it is important to take into account the content that adolescents are watching (what values, social role, etc.) and on the other hand, the context they are watching it in. That is to say, the most direct socialization agents (parents and teachers) mediate and more or less shape the protective "glasses" that the adolescent boy or girl uses to watch television or to use the Internet.

Consequences of Violence for the Victims

Besides possible physical injury, victims of dating violence suffer very deep psychological upset and suffering which is perceived by adolescents as more serious than any physical trauma. Also, both adolescent aggressors and victims involved in dating gender violence usually present symptoms of depression, ideas related to suicide, eating disorders (for example, anorexia or bulimia), low self-esteem, low satisfaction with life, substance abuse (alcohol or other drugs), behavioral and academic problems at school (for example, low performance) and general impairment of physical and mental conditions. In other words, violent adolescent dating relationships have serious psycho-social and health consequences for both victims and aggressors (Muñoz-Rivas & cols., 2007; Ortega, Ortega-Rivera & Sánchez, 2008).

However, this psycho-social maladjustment could be the cause and not only the consequence of being an aggressor or of suffering victimization in adolescent dating relationships. For example, drug and alcohol abuse can be a consequence of being an adolescent aggressor and victim in a dating relationship, but it can also be a risk factor in the sense that it leads to the unleashing of violent behaviors and reduces awareness of risk situations that facilitate aggression. In this sense, low self-esteem, symptoms of depression, anxiety, low satisfaction with life, drug consumption and behavioral problems at school, among others seem to be risk factors for committing violence as well as suffering it in affective relations in adolescence. A very important aspect to highlight is that having been a victim of violence from a partner or having close contact with a victim increases the possibility of becoming involved in another abusive relationship (Vézina & Hérbert, 2007).

Therefore, there are two particularly relevant conditions of risk: tendency to justify and to reproduce sexist and violent models which individuals have lived with during childhood and adolescence; and the imbalance of power existing between men and women, on the bases of which stereotypes linked to gender are created and perpetuated. The most conservative beliefs about the traditional roles of men and women are related to the tendency of men to exert violence and to blame women for violence suffered, and that of women to legitimize the attitudes and behaviors of aggressors.

Intervention Steps: Recommendations for Parents and Teachers

Parents

Some parents can detect one or several signs of abuse, like those described in previous pages, in the behavior of a child and of their partner. However, since adolescents are immersed in a process of distancing and independence from parents, it is easier for a friend or a brother or sister or a teacher to be the figure of support to help them abandon the relationship (Povedano, 2014).

It is, therefore, unadvisable for parents to force a break-up. By doing so, they will be trying to impose a decision about a very intimate aspect of the adolescent's life at a vital time, when one of the aspects of identity affirmation they are trying to assert is making their own decisions. It is necessary to keep lines and spaces open for communication to avoid judgments, to show (including the romantic relationship itself) that love is to do with behaviors and not just feelings and to look for professional help if necessary.

Some examples of the objectives of family intervention are provided below;

- To establish open unbiased communication with the young person suffering dating violence.
- To analyze the myths that sustain unhealthy dating relationships and demonstrate that love is related to behaviors not just feelings.
- To provide tools for solving conflicts that will allow an adolescent to leave a violent relationship through their own decision.

Teachers

As in the case of fathers and mothers, teachers are significant and close to adolescents, and ultimately they are important behavioral models in inter-gender relations and solving conflicts.

For this reason, it is also necessary for teachers and educational centers to generally take on responsibility for the equal standards of relationships and prevention on all levels: detecting and helping find solutions and alternatives in the cases already established, incorporating in the curriculum a critical analysis of the social myths and beliefs that sustain gender-based violence, making a special reference to the gender stereotype that male and female teachers as well as boys and girls live by.

Some examples of the objectives of an intervention program in the educational context are proposed below:

- To train adolescents to be able to detect and recognize physical, psychological, sexual and financial abuse (information about behaviors that can signify the start of exaggerated control or violence).
- To work on coeducation or education in equality values with respect to male and female genders to help prevent the development of beliefs in domination and control over women and "machista" behaviors related to the devaluation of women.
- To raise teachers' awareness that they can become reference adults for adolescents who experience a situation of abuse in their parents' at home, and who initiate a relationship with a partner where there is all likelihood that they will repeat the pattern of the relations they have seen within the family as aggressors or victims. 3703

REFERENCES

Arriaga, X. B. & Foshee, V. (2004). Adolescent dating violence: Do adolescents following their friends', or their parents' footsteps? *Journal of Interpersonal Violence*, *19*, 162–184.

Barnett, O. W., Miller-Perrin, C. L. & Perrin, R. D. (1997). *Family violence across the lifespan: An introduction*. London: Sage.

Billingham, R. E., Bland, R. & Leary, A. (1999). Dating violence at three time periods: 1976, 1992, and 1996. *Psychological Report*, *85*, 574–580.

Bronfenbrenner, U. (1979). *The ecology of human development.* Cambridge, Mass: Harvard University Press.

Capaldi, D. M., Dishion, T. J., Stoolmiller, M. & Yoerger, K. (2001). Aggression toward female partners by at-risk young men: The contribution of male adolescent friendships. *Developmental Psychology, 31*(1), 61–73.

Cleveland, H., Herrera, V. & Stuewig, J. (2003). Abusive males and abused females in adolescent relationships: Risk factor similarity and dissimilarity and the role of relationship seriousness. *Journal of Family Violence, 18*(6), 325–339.

Cornelius, T. L. & Resseguie, N. (2007). Primary and secondary prevention programs for dating violence: A review of the literature. *Aggression and Violent Behavior, 12*, 364–375.

Díaz-Aguado, M. J. & Carvajal, M. I. (2010). *Igualdad y prevención de la violencia de género en la adolescencia.* Madrid: Ministerio de Igualdad y Universidad Complutense de Madrid.

Estévez, E., Povedano, A., Jiménez, T. I. & Musitu, G. (2012). Aggression in Adolescence: A Gender Perspective. In F. Columbus (Ed.), *Psychology Aggression: New Research* (pp. 37-57). New York: Nova Science Publishers.

Foshee, V. A., Bauman, K. E., Linder, F., Rice, J. & Wilcher, R. (2007). Typologies of adolescent dating violence: Identifying typologies of adolescent dating violence perpetration. *Journal of Interpersonal Violence, 22*, 498-519.

Foshee, V. A., Ennett, S. T., Bauman, K. E., Benefield, T. & Suchindran, C. (2005). The association between family violence and adolescent dating violence onset. Does it vary by race, socioeconomic status, and family structure? *The Journal of Early Adolescence, 23*, 317–344.

Gerbner, G., Gross, L., Morgan, M. & Signorielli, N. (1994). Growing up with television: The cultivation perspective. In J. Bryant & D. Zillmann (Eds.), *Media effects* (pp. 17–41). Hillsdale, NJ: Erlbaum.

Gracia, E. & Herrero, J. (2006). Acceptability of domestic violence against women in the European Union: A multilevel analysis. *Journal of epidemiology and community health, 60*(2), 123-129.

Heise, L. L. (1998). Violence against women an integrated, ecological framework. *Violence against women, 4*(3), 262-290.

Herrera, M. C., Expósito, F. & Moya, M. (2012). Negative reactions of men to the loss of power in gender relations: Lilith vs. Eve. *The European journal of psychology applied to legal context, 4*(1), 17.

Hunnicutt, G. (2009). Varieties of patriarchy and violence against women: Resurrecting "patriarchy" as a theoretical tool. *Violence against women.*

Janoff-Bulman, R. & Frieze, I. H. (1983). A theoretical perspective for understanding reactions to victimization. *Journal of Social issues*, *39*(2), 1-17.

Lewis, S. F. & Fremouw, W. (2001). Dating violence: A critical review of the literature. *Clinical Psychology Review*, *21*, 105–127.

Lila, M., Gracia, E. & Murgui, S. (2013). Psychological adjustment and victim-blaming among intimate partner violence offenders: The role of social support and stressful life events. *The European Journal of Psychology Applied to Legal Context*, *5*(2), 147-153.

Muñoz-Rivas, M. J., Grana, J. L., O'Leary, D. K. & González, M. P. (2007). Aggression in adolescent dating relationships: Prevalence, justification, and health consequences. *Journal of Adolescent Health*, *40*, 298–304.

Ortega, R., Ortega-Rivera, J. & Sánchez, V. (2008). Violencia sexual entre compañeros y violencia en parejas adolescentes. *International Journal of Psychology and Psychological Therapy*, *8*, 63-72.

Povedano, A. (2013). Violencia de género en el noviazgo. In E. Estévez (coord.), *Los problemas en la adolescencia: respuestas y sugerencias para padres y educadores* (pp. 211-232). Madrid: Síntesis.

Povedano, A. (2014). *Violencia de género en la adolescencia.* Málaga: IC Editorial.

Povedano, A., Jiménez, T. I. & Valdivieso, L. (2013). Violencia en parejas adolescentes. In G. Musitu (coord.), *Adolescencia y familia: Nuevos retos en el Siglo XXI* (pp. 127-150). México: Trillas.

Povedano, A., Monreal, M. C. & Martínez, B. (2014). Ecological model of factors associated with dating violence. *Journal of Educators, Traders and Teachers*, *5*(3), 105-114.

Povedano, A., Muñiz, M, Cuesta, P. & Musitu, G. (2015). *Educación para la igualdad de género. Un modelo de evaluación*. Madrid: FAD.

Sokoloff, N. J. & Dupont, I. (2005). Domestic violence at the intersections of race, class, and gender challenges and contributions to understanding violence against marginalized women in diverse communities. *Violence against women*, *11*(1), 38-64.

UN. General Assembly Resolution (1993). *Declaration on the elimination of violence against women*. Document A/RES/48/104. UN: New York.

Vézina, J. & Hérbert, M. (2007). Risk factors for victimization in romantic relationships of young women. A review of empirical studies and implications for prevention. Trauma, *Violence, and Abuse*, *8*(1), 33–66.

Walker, L. E. (1977). Battered women and learned helplessness. *Victimology*.
White, J. W. (2002). Gendered aggression across the lifespan. In J. Worrell (Ed.), *Encyclopedia of gender*. New York: Academic Press.

In: Antisocial Behavior ISBN: 978-1-53612-954-0
Editors: Abby Dobson and Peter Talbot © 2017 Nova Science Publishers, Inc.

Chapter 4

ANTISOCIAL BEHAVIOR IN SCHOOLS: PRIMARY CHARACTERISTICS AND INTERVENTION STRATEGIES

***Estefanía Estévez*[1] *and María-Jesús Cava*[2]**
[1]Universidad Miguel Hernández de Elche, Alicante, Spain
[2]Universidad de Valencia, Spain

ABSTRACT

In the school context, some children and adolescents show particular behavioral problems which are inappropriate for their age and have negative consequences for others or themselves. In this regard, one of the problems that currently generates more concern in society is antisocial behavior in educational settings, and especially situations known as bullying. These acts, mostly committed by adolescents, have an increasing prevalence and serious consequences for victims and aggressors, and contaminate the general social environment at school. This short communication addresses these topics, defines some of the main behavioral problems in adolescence in the school environment, including bullying, as well as the main characteristics of aggressors and victims involved in such situations, and the role of bystanders. In addition, an outline is given of some intervention strategies for treating and preventing the different problems of behavior at school.

Behavioral Problems during Adolescence at School

Problem behaviors that may occur in schools are very varied and diversely defined. However, behavior in children and adolescents can be broadly defined as problematic when it involves some type of harm to themselves or others. Harm to themselves includes those behaviors that make their normal development difficult or which prevent them from having an appropriate relation with their social environment. So, high impulsivity, constant hyperactivity or a continual lack of attention to academic activities can be problematic because they hinder students' learning process and in some cases their interpersonal relations. These behaviors will lead to more or less serious problems depending on their duration, intensity and frequency. Other problem behaviors also entail some type of negative consequence or harm to other people, as in the case of physical or verbal aggressions or damage to property. Some of the most frequent problem behaviors in children and adolescents (Armas, 2010; Connor, 2002; Hong & Espelage, 2012; Salmivalli, 2010) are described below.

Attention Deficit Hyperactivity Disorder

Initially called Attention Deficit Disorder (ADD), the term currently used is Attention Deficit Hyperactivity Disorder (ADHD). This syndrome is characterized by lack of attention, impulsivity and an excessive level of activity. For this disorder to be diagnosed, these behaviors have to be clinically significant and manifest in at least two different contexts. There is currently some controversy about the excessive use of this diagnosis, and in fact it is very important to differentiate between children that have a determined feature of hyperactivity and those who actually have ADHD. Although early and accurate diagnosis can help children with attention and hyperactivity problems, difficulties can arise as a consequence of incorrect early "labeling." Furthermore, the way of educating hyperactive children can largely contribute to decreasing the intensity of their problem behaviors, and it is fundamental to adapt to their educational needs. These children need limits and clear rules that are applied with care and affection. Collaboration between the family and school, and standardizing criteria and educational guidelines are necessary in order to favor students' adaptation to school.

Oppositional Defiant Disorder

Some behaviors of disobedience in infancy and also some defiant behaviors towards authority during adolescence are part of the normal evolutionary development of children and adolescents. However, the oppositional defiant disorder arises when the frequency and intensity of these defiant behaviors are so high that they seriously impair relationships with parents and teachers. This disorder is characterized by recurring oppositional behaviors (continual refusal to do tasks required by parents or teachers), defiance towards authority, disobedience and animosity. These behaviors usually start in the family environment and later extend to other contexts like school. Although authority and rules are constantly defied, the fundamental rights of others are respected; theft, intimidation, cruelty or destruction of other people's property do not occur. Although the causes of these behaviors are numerous, some factors at school can contribute to this behavior either continuing and becoming more serious or gradually disappearing. In the event that this so-called *pathological disobedience* continues in adolescence, it tends to evolve towards dissocial disorder.

Antisocial Disorder

This disorder is characterized by frequent aggressive behaviors, like insults and fights, as well as by theft, cruelty towards people or animals, unjustified absences from school, running away from home and continually breaking the rules at home or at school. It is, therefore, a persistent behavior of violating other people's basic rights and the social norms corresponding to that age, where adolescents always engage in anti-social acts and even in criminal acts. This fact seriously impairs the psycho-social adjustment of a child or an adolescent, as well as their adjustment to their most immediate environment. These problematic behaviors are a consequence of numerous individual or family and social causes. In these situations, the most effective action is interdisciplinary interventions, which are made on all levels - individual, family and school. It is considered a major problem, since it has been confirmed that approximately half the adolescents with anti-social disorder persist in this behavior in adulthood. It is not, therefore, a transitory antisocial behavior occurring in the adolescent stage as in the majority of cases of peer abuse or violence, which systematically ceases in late adolescence.

Peer Violence and Bullying

Peer violence refers to all physical, verbal or relational aggressions between students (Hong & Espelage, 2012). These aggressions can be isolated events or persistent, recurring and always directed at the same victim. When these aggressions are committed with the clear purpose of causing harm to a specific victim, they are persistent over time and there is a clear imbalance of power between victim and aggressors, this is bullying (Cava, 2013). Physical and verbal aggressions consist of direct violence, as there is a face to face confrontation between aggressors and the victim.

In relational aggressions, there is no direct confrontation with the victim; harm is caused through the victim's circle of friends and through their perception of belonging to a group, by using social exclusion, rejection and spreading malicious rumors. A recent addition to these traditional types of aggression is the use of new technologies.

Cyberbullying shares the basic characteristics of traditional bullying (repeated harm to the victim, imbalance of power and the victim's difficulty in avoiding the situation), and it also has its own particular characteristics (Kowalski, Giumetti, Schroeder, & Lattanner, 2014; Ortega-Baron, Buelga, & Cava, 2016). In this type of bullying, the aggressor's anonymity is frequent, the aggression suffered is quickly spread through social networks and the victim has a greater sensation of vulnerability, since they do not feel safe in any place at any time (Buelga, Iranzo, Cava, & Torralba, 2015; Kowalski et al., 2014).

Main Characteristics of Aggressors, Victims and Bystanders

Although early research about *bullying* focused on analyzing the profile of aggressors and victims individually, it is now considered a group phenomenon where other students intervene directly or indirectly, acting or remaining passive (Hong & Espelage, 2012). There are, therefore, three different basic roles to be considered: aggressors, victims, and bystanders (Salmivalli, 2010). Group dynamics are established between these three different roles which contribute to bullying situations being maintained. It is, therefore, important to know their main characteristics.

Aggressors

Bullies are often characterized by showing high levels of impulsivity, a strong need to dominate others, positive beliefs about the use of violence and low empathy with victims (Evans, Heriot, and Friedman, 2002; Olweus, 2005). Moreover, they tend to be physically stronger than their victims and have more difficulties in accepting and following the established social rules. Other studies have shown a close link between a negative attitude towards formal authority (teachers, school, and police) and violent behaviour in adolescence (Estévez, Jiménez, & Cava, 2016). Research has also documented that bullies tend to get low scores in self-esteem in the school and family domains, but high scores in social self-esteem (Andreou, 2000; Estévez, Martínez, & Musitu, 2006; O'Moore & Kirkman, 2001).

Victims

Although some vulnerability factors are indicated to increase the likelihood of a student suffering *bullying*, it is true that in certain circumstances any student can be a victim. Sometimes, it is physical differences, sexual orientation, religion or culture that increase the likelihood of suffering *bullying*. In other cases, it is the victim's lack of assertiveness or their social isolation in the classroom, which is a determining element. Their isolation can be prior to bullying, since some victims already experience social rejection, but it can also be a consequence of isolation that arises after suffering bullying (Povedano, Cava, Monreal, Varela, & Musitu, 2015).

Victimization in schools implies a high threat to the psychological wellbeing of children and adolescents, since it is an extremely stressful interpersonal experience, and in fact, many investigations have repeatedly shown how victimized students exhibit serious psychosomatic symptoms and poor psychological adjustment. Moreover, these problems seem to persist over time and many of these students need to ask, ultimately, for help and support from mental health professionals (Guterman, Hahm, and Cameron, 2002). In this sense, for example, Guterman and colleagues observed that the victims of bullying presented depressive symptoms, anxiety and stress problems even a year after the last violent encounter. It has been proved that victims of bullying at school tend to have poorer self-esteem, tend to show more psychological distress, and score higher in the feeling of loneliness and suicide ideation.

Bystanders

The term "bystanders" is used to refer to those students who do not bully the victim but are aware of the situation (Hong & Espelage, 2012). These students frequently stay on the sidelines and do not help the victim. This passive reaction can be partly explained by their fear of becoming new victims and from being afraid of confronting their aggressors. This passiveness in their environment (sometimes including some teachers) makes the abuser or abusers (bully/bullies) feel stronger with respect to the victim, which contributes to the bullying continuing. In fact, one aspect of bullying intervention strategies that is receiving more and more attention is that of mobilizing bystanders so that they support victims of bullying.

Prevention and Intervention from the School

All the problem behaviors described represent an important challenge for schools and imply the need to carry out interventions for their prevention or elimination once they have occurred. These interventions should maintain a global focus, since changing a student's behavior often requires changing their relations with other people from their family, school and social circle (Armas, 2010; Conoley & Goldstein, 2004; Salmivalli, 2010; Walker, Colvin, & Ramsey, 1995). It is possible for schools to prevent and intervene in many of the problems through different strategies, thereby improving social integration of all students and favoring a suitable climate of coexistence. These interventions are not only positive for students with difficulties, but also for the rest of the students, for teachers and for families.

Nevertheless, it is true that prevention and intervention in behavioral problems and bullying in schools are at the same time necessary but complicated issues. Authors like Rigby (2012) point out that some *impediments* or difficulties when dealing with violent situations in educational establishments are related to "a serious imbalance of attention being given to different aspects of the problem, with relatively little attention being paid to direct methods of intervention in actual cases of bullying." The reasons argued by Rigby are given below:

1. Actual cases of bullying are not being dealt with well. Only a minority of children being bullied go to teachers for help. Overall, teachers are

unable to help more than half of them – and much less than half of the adolescent students who need help.

2. Most schools exhort students who are being bullied to tell. Most students do not. Given the reluctance many students have to inform and the low level of confidence that many students have about whether teachers can help, this is not surprising.
3. Meanwhile a good deal of attention is being directed in some schools toward promoting constructive and socially positive ways in which all children can relate to each other happily. What is sometimes not recognized is that most children do that. They do not bully, or do so rarely; most students are not bullied, except quite occasionally. Programs to improve the general belief system of the school may help, but for the most part their impact on bullying is limited. The behavior of the minority of children who continually engage in bullying or suffer from being bullied will be affected to a minor degree.
4. Crucially, as many researchers have pointed out, the vast majority of cases of bullying involve a small minority of students, as either bullies, victims or bully-victims, and the causes of the bullying often lie outside the reach of the school.
5. Finally, teachers and often counselors are largely uninformed about what can in fact be done to address actual cases of bullying.

Even so, in the school context there is an attempt to carry out different strategies to prevent problem behaviors in students and to intervene once they have occurred. These strategies should rely on support from the whole educational community, with everyone being aware of their usefulness for favoring school coexistence and the adequate psychosocial development of all students. It is useful to combine different strategies and for them to be continuous over time, by monitoring and evaluating their effectiveness in each school. Some intervention strategies are described below.

The Importance of Prevention and Sensitization

Prevention has unquestionable advantages in the school environment (Garaigordobil & Oñederra, 2010; Orpinas & Horne, 2006; Torrego, 2013). Prevention decreases the incidence of problem behaviors which can negatively affect students' psycho-social adjustment. Furthermore, these interventions entail lower costs in resources and their effects are broader as they influence a greater number of students compared to interventions in problems that have already been detected. Also, in an educational context, prevention has a special sense and usefulness since many of the prevention strategies focus on emotional education and foster students' personal and social resources, thereby favoring their cognitive, affective and social development. However, although these advantages are significant, not all schools are fully aware of the importance of developing intervention proposals that address the prevention of problem behaviors and the improvement of coexistence in the school.

In some schools only learning and curriculum content are given any attention; improvement in interpersonal relations among students and between students and teachers are perceived as secondary or even unnecessary. In other cases, some parents or students are the ones who consider that these interventions are not useful for them and see them as a waste of time. However, these interventions have positive effects for all students, not only for those who have difficulties. Therefore, it is very important to raise awareness about their usefulness throughout the educational community beforehand, so that the time invested may later be perceived as having an impact on improving the quality of social relations and the education process itself. When time and effort is devoted to improving coexistence in school, disruptive behaviors in the classroom decrease, students' motivation in the learning process increases and teachers also become more motivated.

On the other hand, it is also important that everyone should be aware of how certain problems in schools affect everyone and not only those directly involved. For example, when there is a school bullying situation in a school, the climate generated has an impact on the rest of students, who may be afraid of being the aggressor's next target or may feel guilty in the event of not helping a victim. In this sense, informing and sensitizing parents, teachers and students about the negative consequences of all types of violence, promoting zero tolerance towards all these types of violence and favoring victim support can decrease school violence in educational establishments (Cava, 2013).

One intervention strategy that helps students to solve their conflicts peacefully and also contributes to preventing different interpersonal problems is the creation of a student mediation team in the school (Boqué, 2002; Torrego, 2005). Mediation teams consist of students who have been previously trained in mediating and they are generally coordinated by several teachers, also trained in the basic mediation principles. These basic principles include the voluntary participation of the conflicting parties in the mediation process, their active participation during the sessions and their commitment to listen respectfully to the other conflicting party in the mediation process, and to maintain confidentiality with respect to the ideas, feelings, needs and interests expressed (Cava, 2009).

Having a mediation team in a school is not only useful for some students who manage to solve certain interpersonal conflicts with its help, but it also provides important benefits for the student mediators who are members of the team and for the whole educational community. Student mediators develop social competences, such as empathy or active listening, which can be useful in other contexts and undoubtedly contribute to personal development. What is more, having a mediation team available to the whole educational community is a way of expressing the importance given to the values related to the culture of peace, coexistence based on respect for others and peaceful solution to conflicts. Although students may not use the mediation team, by implementing these types of projects, they all perceive that the school gives importance to these values.

Intervention Protocols in Situations of School Violence

Although the incidence of anti-social behavior and *bullying* situations in schools decreases considerably when preventive measures are taken, it is necessary to also have an intervention protocol in response to possible cases. (Cava, 2013). In this way, when a student, teacher or father/mother discovers that there could be a *bullying*, or *cyberbullying* situation, if there is a clear intervention protocol, and more importantly it is known to everyone, this will make it easier to adopt adequate, fast and effective measures. It is fundamental for this intervention protocol to be known to everyone, because although there is one, on occasions it is not followed or not followed adequately. Although intervention protocols can differ from one center to another, the following steps are implemented in the majority of them.

1. *Victim support and emergency measures*. The first actions should focus on protecting the possible victim safety and offering them safety. Although on occasions *bullying* is not confirmed, possible cases reported should be listened to, attended and analyzed. While a case is being analyzed and its nature and seriousness are determined, some primary emergency measures should be carried out which will increase the feeling of safety and support in the possible victim, such as not leaving them alone or increasing vigilance in the center,

2. *Gathering information from different sources and communicating with families.* It is important to gather as much information as possible about the situation as soon as possible. To do so, individual interviews are carried out with all the students involved, and occasionally with other students and some teachers. On the basis of these interviews, it will be determined whether or not there is a case of *bullying,* the seriousness of the situation, its duration, the context it occurred in and exactly who is involved and to what extent. Communication with the families should be clear and complete, and they should be assured of the school's support and interest in avoiding any type of situation of school violence and bullying, as well as the intention to analyze the case in depth and to search for a solution while counting on their collaboration.
3. *Application of disciplinary measures.* Although the exact measures to be applied will depend on the seriousness of the case and the specific regulations of the center, it is recommended that these measures do not just involve punishment. If they only include disciplinary proceedings and students being temporarily expelled from the school, it is likely that the violent behaviors will be repeated once the student or students return. To avoid this, schools should create an Intervention Plan that includes the victim and the aggressors as well as the rest of the students.
4. *Creating an Intervention Plan and communicating it to the families.* This Intervention Plan can be carried out in collaboration with the school's educational authority and the specialists that work there. Once the Intervention Plan has been created, it should be communicated to the students and their families, since their involvement is essential. In the case of the aggressor, it is advisable that their family is made to see that the difficulties of their child will become even more serious if they are not dealt with as soon as possible. Although they may be reticent and have defensive attitudes, usually the best way to achieve their collaboration is to avoid laying the blame on them and to offer them orientation and support. With these students, the intervention to be carried out should combine the supervision and sanction of their aggressive behaviors, for example, actions directed at developing appropriate social behaviors. The aggressor should understand why their behavior is unacceptable and it is necessary to help them develop alternative behaviors.

Intervention with victims usually focuses primarily on offering them safety and support and helping them overcome the situation they have experienced and giving them the personal and social resources which will help them to avoid these situations. Some of the aspects worked on with victims are: how to respond before possible new attacks from aggressors, how to respond assertively to fellow students, how to avoid dangerous situations and how to ask for help. With the rest of students it is a good idea to increase sensitization and make them aware that they could also contribute a lot to these situations being avoided if they reject the aggressor's behavior and show support to the victim.

5. *Monitoring and valuation of the Intervention Plan.* It is just as important to carry out a post monitoring and valuation of the Intervention Plan itself. At the time the Intervention Plan is created, it is recommended to fix a period for its post evaluation. This evaluation could be carried out through interviews with teachers, students and families, analyzing together the current relations among students, if there are any difficulties and how they each feel at school. These students' teachers can provide information about their behavior in the classroom. Once monitoring has been completed, if difficulties in coexistence are still observed, a new Intervention Plan can be implemented which will lead to overcoming the problem situation.

REFERENCES

Andreou, E. (2000). Bully/Victim problems and their association with psychological constructs in 8-to 12-year old Greek school children. *Aggressive Behavior, 26*, 49-56.

Armas, M. (2010). *Prevención e intervención ante problemas de conducta. Estrategias para centros educativos y familias [Prevention and intervention for behavioral problems. Strategies for educational centers and families]*. Madrid: Wolters Kluwer.

Boqué, M. C. (2002). *Guía de mediación escolar. [School Mediation Guide.]* Barcelona: Octaedro.

Buelga, S., Iranzo, B., Cava, M. J., & Torralba, E. (2015). Psychological profile of adolescent cyberbullying aggressors. *International Journal of Social Psychology, 30 (2),*382-406.

Cava, M. J. (2009). La utilidad de la mediación como estrategia de resolución y prevención de conflictos en el ámbito escolar. *Informació Psicològica, [The utility of mediation as a strategy for conflict resolution and prevention in the school setting. Psychological Information] 95*, 15-26.

Cava, M.J. (2013). El acoso escolar: cuando la escuela no es un lugar seguro. En E. Estévez (coord.), *Los problemas en la adolescencia: Repuestas y sugerencias para padres y profesionales* [Bullying: when school is not a safe place. In E. Estévez (coord.), *Problems in adolescence: Answers and suggestions for parents and professionals*] (pp. 97-120). Madrid: Síntesis.

Connor, D. F. (2002). *Aggression and antisocial behavior in children and adolescents*. New York: Guilford Press.

Conoley, J.C. & Goldstein, A. P. (2004). *School violence intervention.* London: Guilford Press.

Estévez, E., Jiménez, T., & Cava, M.J. (2016). A cross-cultural study in Spain and Mexico on school aggression in adolescence: examining the role of individual, family and school variables. *Cross-cultural Research. 50(2),* 1-31.

Estévez, E., Martínez, B., & Musitu, G. (2006). La autoestima en adolescentes agresores y víctimas en la escuela: La perspectiva multidimensional [Self-esteem in aggressors and victims of school violence: the multidimensional perspective]. *Intervención Psicosocial, 12,* 32-41.

Evans, M., Heriot, S. A., & Friedman, A. G. (2002). A behavioural pattern of irritability, hostility and inhibited empathy in children. *Clinical Child Psychology and Psychiatry, 7*, 211-224.

Garaigordobil, M. & Oñederra, J. A. (2010). *La violencia entre iguales. Revisión teórica y estrategias de intervención. [Violence between equals. Theoretical review and intervention strategies.]* Madrid: Pirámide.

Guterman, N. B., Hahm, H. C., & Cameron, M. (2002). Adolescent victimization and subsequent use of mental health counselling services. *Journal of adolescent Health, 30*, 336-345.

Hong, J. S. & Espelage, D. L. (2012). A review of research on bullying and peer victimization in school: An ecological system analysis. *Aggression and Violent Behavior, 17*, 311-322.

Kowalski, R.M., Giumetti, G.W., Schroeder, A.N., & Lattanner, M.R. (2014). Bullying in the Digital Age: A Critical Review and Meta-analysis of Cyberbullying Research among Youth. *Psychological Bulletin, 140(4*), 1073-1137.

Olweus, D. (1998). *Conductas de acoso y amenaza entre escolares. [Harassment and threat behavior among schoolchildren.]* Madrid: Morata.

Olweus, D. (2005). Bullying at school: data and intervention. *IX International Meeting about Biology and Sociology of Violence: Violence and School.* Valencia (Spain).

O'Moore, M., & Kirkham, C. (2001). Self-steem and its relationships to bullying behaviour. *Aggressive Behavior, 27*, 269-283.

Orpinas, P. & Horne, A. M. (2006). *Bullying prevention: Creating a positive school climate and developing social competence.* Washington, DC, US: American Psychological Association.

Ortega, R. (1998). *La convivencia escolar: qué es y cómo abordarla. [School coexistence: what it is and how to approach it.]* Sevilla: Junta de Andalucía.

Ortega-Baron, J., Buelga, S., & Cava, M.J. (2016). The Influence of School and Family Environment on Adolescent Victims of Cyberbullying. *Comunicar, 46,* 57-65.

Povedano, A., Cava, M. J., Monreal, M. C., Varela, R., & Musitu, G.(2015) Victimization, loneliness, overt and relational violence at the school from a gender perspective. *International Journal of Clinical and Health Psychology (1*), 44-51.

Rigby, K (2012). *Bullying Interventions in Schools: Six Basic Approaches.* Oxford, UK: Blackwell Publishing.

Salmivalli, C. (2010). Bullying and the peer group: A review. *Aggression and Violent Behavior, 15*, 112-120.

Torrego, J. C. (2005). *Mediación de conflictos en instituciones educativas. Manual para la formación de mediadores. [Mediation of conflicts in educational institutions. Manual for the training of mediators.]* Madrid: Narcea.

Torrego, J. C. (2013). *La ayuda entre iguales para mejorar la convivencia escolar. Manual para la formación de alumnos ayudantes. [The help among peers to improve school coexistence. Manual for the training of student assistants.]* Madrid: Narcea.

Walker, H., Colvin, G., & Ramsey, E. (1995). *Antisocial behavior in school: Strategies and best practices.* Pacific Grove, CA: Brooks/Cole Publishing Company.

BIBLIOGRAPHY

African American psychology: from Africa to America

LCCN	2013016472
Type of material	Book
Personal name	Belgrave, Faye Z., author.
Main title	African American psychology: from Africa to America / Faye Z. Belgrave, Virginia Commonwealth University, Kevin W. Allison, Virginia Commonwealth University
Edition	Third Edition.
Published/Produced	Los Angeles, California: SAGE Publications, [2014]
Description	xviii, 644 pages; 26 cm
ISBN	9781412999540 (pbk.: alk. paper)
LC classification	E185.625 .B425 2014
Related names	Allison, Kevin W., author.
Contents	Introduction to African American psychology -- African-centered psychology -- Self-attributes and identity -- Race and racism -- Kinship and family -- Education and work -- Neighborhoods and communities -- Interpersonal and close relationships -- Cognition, learning, and language -- Religion and spirituality -- Life-span development -- Health, illness, and disability -- Psychosocial adaptation and mental health -- Drug use and abuse -- Prosocial and antisocial behavior.

Subjects	African Americans--Psychology. African Americans--Socialization. African Americans--Social conditions. Afrocentrism. United States--Civilization--African influences. Africa--Civilization. Africa, West--Civilization.
Notes	Includes bibliographical references (pages 513-590) and indexes.

Antisocial behavior & crime: contributions of developmental and evaluation research to prevention and intervention

LCCN	2011940025
Type of material	Book
Main title	Antisocial behavior & crime: contributions of developmental and evaluation research to prevention and intervention / Thomas Bliesener, Andreas Beelmann, Mark Stemmler, editors.
Published/Created	Cambridge, MA: Hogrefe; Ashland, Ohio: Distributed by Hogrefe Pub., c2012.
Description	xviii, 381 p.: ill.; 24 cm.
ISBN	9780889374249 0889374244
LC classification	HV6080 .A668 2012
Variant title	Antisocial behavior and crime
Related names	Bliesener, Thomas. Beelmann, Andreas. Stemmler, M. (Mark)
Contents	In honor of Friedrich Lösel / Thomas Bliesener, Andreas Beelmann and Mark Stemmler -- Developmental courses of antisocial behaviors. Environmental, genetic and epigenetic influences on the developmental origins of aggression and other disruptive behaviors / Richard E Tremblay -- Subtypes of aggressive behaviors: etiologies, development, and consequences / Frank Vitaro and Mara Brendgen -- Developmental sequence and pathways towards serious delinquency and substance use / Rolf Loeber, Helene Raskin White and Jeffery D Burke -- Persistent

juvenile offenders / Thomas Bliesener -- Risk and protective factors in antisocial behaviors. Protective and promotive factors in the development of offending / David P Farrington and Maria M Ttofi -- Family factors in the development of antisocial behavior / Lea Pulkkinen -- Social sources of crime propensity: a study of the collective efficacy of families, schools, and neighborhoods / Per-Olof H Wikström -- Media consumption and violence in schools / Franz Streng -- Crime prevention, offender treatment, and rehabilitation. The scientific foundation of prevention: the status quo and future challenges for developmental crime prevention crime prevention / Andreas Beelmann -- Measuring conflict of interest in prevention and intervention research: a feasibility study / Manuel Eisner and David Humphreys -- Effective interventions for juvenile offenders: using meta-analysis to bridge from research to practice / Mark W Lipsey -- Offender resistance policing (ODP): less prison and more evidence in rehabilitating offenders / Lawrence W Sherman -- Risk management and criminal justice. Violence risk assessment: things that I have learned so far / David J Cooke -- Comprehensive risk management instruments for serious and violent young offenders: challenges and advantages / Raymond R Carrado -- Forensic psychological assessment in the criminal justice system:development and perspectives in Germany / Rudolf Egg -- Young offenders and legal competencies / Ronald Roesch -- Research methods in development criminology. The development of delinquent behavior: variable- and person-oriented methods of analysis / Alexander von Eye, Richard M Lerner, Jacqueline V Lerner and Edmond P Bowers -- Latent growth curve modeling and the study of problem behavior in girls / Mark Stemmler and Anne C Peterson -- Evaluating a national program: effects of No Child Left Behind on math achievement in the United States / Thomas D Cook, Manyee Wong, and Peter Steiner -- Principles of

	symmetry in evaluation research with implications for offender treatment / Werner W Wittmann.
Subjects	Criminal behavior.
	Antisocial personality disorders.
	Developmental psychology.
Notes	Includes bibliographical references and index.

Antisocial behavior: causes, correlations and treatments

LCCN	2010043928
Type of material	Book
Main title	Antisocial behavior: causes, correlations and treatments / Rebecca M. Clarke, editor.
Published/Created	New York: Nova Science Publishers, c2011.
Description	x, 201 p.: ill.; 27 cm.
ISBN	9781611228908 (hbk.)
	1611228905 (hbk.)
LC classification	RC555 .A56 2011
Related names	Clarke, Rebecca M.
Subjects	Antisocial personality disorders.
	Antisocial personality disorders--Treatment.
Notes	Includes bibliographical references and index.
Series	Psychology of emotions, motivations and actions
	Psychology of emotions, motivations, and actions series.

Antisocial behavior: etiology, genetic and environmental influences and clinical management

LCCN	2014026715
Type of material	Book
Main title	Antisocial behavior: etiology, genetic and environmental influences and clinical management / editor, Justine H. Gallo.
Published/Produced	New York: Nova Publishers, [2014]
Description	x, 178 pages: illustrations; 26 cm.
ISBN	9781633215214 (hardcover)
LC classification	RC555 .A563 2014
Related names	Gallo, Justine H.
Subjects	Antisocial personality disorders.
	Antisocial personality disorders--Treatment.

Notes	Includes index.
Series	Psychology research progress

Antisocial behavior

LCCN	2011000527
Type of material	Book
Personal name	Spalding, Frank.
Main title	Antisocial behavior / Frank Spalding.
Edition	1st ed.
Published/Created	New York: Rosen Pub., 2012.
Description	48 p.: col. ill.; 24 cm.
ISBN	9781448845859 (library binding)
LC classification	RC555 .S69 2012
Contents	Antisocial behavior during the teen years -- Struggling with antisocial impulses -- When you're the victim: coping with the effects of antisocial behavior -- Pushing back: combating antisocial behavior.
Subjects	Antisocial personality disorders. Antisocial personality disorders--Prevention. Conduct disorders in adolescence.
Notes	Includes bibliographical references (p. 45-46) and index.
Series	Teen mental health

Behavior genetics of psychopathology

LCCN	2014930299
Type of material	Book
Main title	Behavior genetics of psychopathology / Soo Hyun Rhee, Angelica Ronald, editors.
Published/Produced	New York: Springer, [2014]
Description	viii, 344 pages: illustrations; 24 cm.
ISBN	9781461495086 (alk. paper) 1461495083 (alk. paper)
LC classification	QH457 .B4225 2014
Related names	Rhee, Soo Hyun. Ronald, Angelica.
Summary	"As a dynamic, interdisciplinary field, behavior genetics and its evolution are being followed closely by scientists across the psychological and medical

domains. The discoveries surrounding the human genome and the advancement in molecular genetic technologies have led to studies becoming increasingly sophisticated and yielding yet more conclusive and useful results. This is certainly the case in the area of child and adult psychopathology. Behavior Genetics of Psychopathology summarizes the state of the field, examining the role of genes and environment as they affect common neurodevelopmental and psychiatric conditions. Emphasizing key research areas (comorbidities, twin studies, the integration of methods), the book assesses the current literature, offers up-to-date findings, sorts through lingering controversies, and identifies a clear future agenda for the field. Expertly-written chapters focus on issues of general salience that shape behavior genetics of psychopathology, as well as specific disorders of major clinical importance, among them: ADHD: the view from quantitative genetic research. Autism spectrum disorders and their complex heterogeneity Genetic influences on anxiety and depression in childhood and adolescence. Evidence for etiologically-defined subgroups within the construct of antisocial behavior. Sleep and psychopathology: the reasons for their co-occurrence. Behavioral genetic approaches to the etiology of comorbidity. Epigenetics of psychopathology. This combination of timeliness and depth of coverage make Behavior Genetics of Psychopathology a frontline resource for behavior geneticists, psychologists, psychiatrists, and neuroscientists, and is perfectly suited to graduate students looking to join these fields."-- P. 4 of cover.

Contents Attention Deficit Hyperactivity Disorder: insight from quantitative genetic research -- Progress in understanding the causes of autism spectrum disorders and autistic traits: Twin studies from 1977 to the present day -- Genetic influences on depression and anxiety in childhood and adolescence -- Additional Evidence for Meaningful Etiological Distinctions

	within the Broader Construct of Antisocial Behavior -- Sleep and Psychopathology: Quantitative and Molecular Genetic Research on Comorbidity -- Schizophrenia and Bipolar Disorder -- Genetics of Substance Use Disorders -- Behavioral genetic approaches to understand the etiology of comorbidity -- Gene-Environment Interactions (GxE) in Behavioral Genetics -- Epigenetics of Psychopathology -- Future Directions In Genetics Of Psychiatric Disorders.
Subjects	Behavior genetics. Psychology, Pathological. Genetic Predisposition to Disease. Mental Disorders--genetics. Genetics, Behavioral. Behavior genetics. Psychology, Pathological.
Notes	Includes bibliographical references and index.
Series	Advances in behavior genetics; 2 Advances in behavior genetics; 2.

Bio-psycho-social perspectives on interpersonal violence

LCCN	2010001158
Type of material	Book
Main title	Bio-psycho-social perspectives on interpersonal violence / Martha Frias-Armenta and Victor Corral-Verdugo, editors.
Published/Created	New York: Nova Science Publishers, c2010.
Description	xiv, 376 p.: ill.; 27 cm.
ISBN	9781616681593 (hardcover) 1616681594 (hardcover)
LC classification	BF575.A3 B566 2010
Related names	Frías Armenta, Martha. Corral Verdugo, Víctor.
Contents	Aggression, risk-taking, and alternative life-history strategies: the behavioral ecology of social deviance / Aurelio José Figueredo and W. Jake Jacobs -- Executive functions, attention, and juvenile delinquency / Martha Frías-Armenta ... [et al.] -- A study of personality traits in undergraduates:

Alexythymial and its relationship to the psychopathic deviate / José Moral de la Rubia -- Self-control, self-regulation, and juvenile delinquency / Martha Frías-Armenta ... [et al.] -- Child maltreatment, self-regulation, and parenting / José Concepción Gaxiola-Romero and Martha Frías-Armenta -- Environmental factors in housing habitability as determinants of family violence / Victor Corral-Verdugo, Martha Frías-Armenta and Daniel González-Lomelí -- The role of family communication and school adjustment in adolescents' violent behavior / María Elena Villarreal-González, Juan Carlos Sánchez-Sosa and Gonzalo Musitu-Ochoa -- Violent offenders: a qualitative study of murderous violence in Venezuela / Alejandro Moreno -- Environmental and personal variables predicting school bullying: a study of Mexican adolescents / Victor Corral-Verdugo ... [et al.] -- Violence in prison: institutional constraints and inmates aggressiveness / Rui Abrunhosa Gonçalves -- Media effects on antisocial behavior in children and adolescents / Pablo Espinoza and Miguel Clemente -- Witnesses to bullying: voices for prevention and intervention in schools / Marcela López, María José Aguilar and Josefina Rubiales -- Methods in psychology & law and criminological research: the assessment of interventions for prevention of crime / Eugenio de Gregorio -- The impact of PPS-VCJ on attitudes and behavior of juveniles placed in centers as a result of judicial measures / Ana M. Martín ... [et al.] -- Juvenile offenders recidivism in Spain: a quantitative revision / Juan García-García, Elena Ortega-Campos and Leticia de la Fuente-Sánchez.

Subjects Violence--Psychological aspects.
Violence--Social aspects.

Notes Includes bibliographical references and index.

Series Psychology of emotions, motivations and actions
Psychology of emotions, motivations, and actions series.

Calli

LCCN	2011007076
Type of material	Book
Personal name	Anderson, Jessica Lee, 1980-
Main title	Calli / Jessica Lee Anderson.
Edition	1st ed.
Published/Created	Minneapolis, Minn.: Milkweed Editions, 2011.
Description	184 p.; 21 cm.
ISBN	9781571317025 (cloth) 9781571316998 (pbk.)
LC classification	PZ7.A53665 Cal 2011
Summary	When fifteen-year-old Calli's two moms take in Cherish, a troubled teenager, and Calli tries to stand up to her antisocial behavior, things quickly begin to spiral downward before Calli can begin to regain some semblance of control.
Subjects	Family problems--Fiction. Foster home care--Fiction. Lesbians--Fiction. Mothers and daughters--Fiction. Interpersonal relations--Fiction.

Classics of criminology

LCCN	2012382067
Type of material	Book
Main title	Classics of criminology / edited by Joseph E. Jacoby, Theresa A. Severance, Alan S. Bruce.
Edition	4th ed.
Published/Created	Long Grove, Ill.: Waveland Press, c2012.
Description	xvi, 688 p.: ill.; 23 cm.
ISBN	9781577667360 (pbk.) 1577667360 (pbk.)
LC classification	HV6779 .C53 2012
Related names	Jacoby, Joseph E. Severance, Theresa A. Bruce, Alan S.
Contents	What is a gang? / Frederick M. Thrasher -- The professional thief; White-collar criminality / Edwin H. Sutherland -- Juvenile delinquency and urban areas /

Clifford R. Shaw and Henry D. McKay -- The criminal and his victim / Hans von Hentig -- Victim-precipitated criminal homicide / Marvin E. Wolfgang -- Delinquency in a birth cohort / Marvin E. Wolfgang, Thorsten Sellin, and Robert Figlio -- Social change and crime: a routine activity approach / Lawrence E. Cohen and Marcus Felson -- Environmental criminology / Paul J. Brantingham and Patricia L. Brantingham -- Characterizing criminal careers / Alfred Blumstein and Jacqueline Cohen -- Crime and deviance over the life course: the salience of adult social bonds / Robert J. Sampson and John H. Laub -- Adolescence-limited and life-course-persistent antisocial behavior: a developmental taxonomy / Terrie E. Moffitt -- The cycle of violence / Cathy Spatz Widom -- Seductions of crime: moral and sensual attractions in doing evil / Jack Katz -- The code of the streets / Elijah Anderson -- An introduction to the principles of morals and legislation / Jeremy Bentham -- Modeling offenders' decisions: a framework for research and policy / Ronald V. Clarke and Derek B. Cornish -- The normal and the pathological / Emile Durkheim -- Class conflict and law / Karl Marx -- Class, state, and crime / Richard Quinney -- Criminal man / Gina Lombroso-Ferrero -- The jukes: a study in crime, pauperism, and heredity / Richard Dugdale -- The American criminal / Ernest A. Hooton / Criminality in adoptees and their adoptive and biological parents: a pilot study / Barry Hutchins and Sarnoff A. Mednick -- Crime and human nature / James Q. Wilson and Richard J. Herrnstein -- Suicide / Emile Durkheim -- Social structure and anomie / Robert K. Merton -- Foundation for a general strain theory of crime and delinquency / Rrobert Agnew -- Culture conflict and crime / Thorsten Sellin -- Differential systems of values / Clifford R. Shaw and Henry D. McKay -- The content of the delinquent subculture / Albert K. Cohen -- Lower class culture as a generating milieu of gang delinquency / Walter B.

Miller -- Techniques of neutralization / Gresham M. Sykes and David Matza -- Differential association / Edwain H. Sutherland -- A differential association-reinforcement theory of criminal behavior / Robert L. Burgess and Ronald L. Akers -- Delinquency and opportunity / Richard A. Cloward and Lloyd E. Ohlin -- Unraveling juvenile delinquency / Sheldon Glueck and Eleanor Glueck -- A control theory of delinquency / Travis Hirschi -- Class in the household: a power-control theory of gender and delinquency / John Hagan, John Simpson, and A. R. Gillis -- A general theory of crime / Michael R. Gottfredson and Travis Hirschi -- The dramatization of evil / Frank Tannenbaum -- Primary and secondary deviation / Edwin Lemert -- Outsiders / Howard S. Beck -- Deviance and moral panics / Stanley Cohen -- The etiology of female crime: a review of the literature / Dorie Klein -- Girls' crime and woman's place: toward a feminist model of female delinquency / Meda Chesney-Lind -- Women's pathways to felony court: feminist theories of lawbreaking and problems of representation / Kathleen Daly -- Of crimes and punishments / Cesare Beccaria -- The challenge of crime in a free society / President's Commission on Law Enforcement and the Administration of Justice -- Doing justice: the choice of punishments / Andrew von Hirsch -- Retributive justice, restorative justice / Howard Zehr -- Restorative justice and a better future / John Braithwaite -- Punishment and social structure / Georg Rusche and Otto Kirchheimer -- The law of vagrancy / William J. Chambliss -- Two models of the criminal process / Herbert L. Packer -- Guilty until proved innocent: wrongful conviction and public policy / C. Ronald Huff, Arye Rattner, and Edward Sagarin -- A sketch of the policeman's "working personality" / Jerome H. Skolnick -- Police control of juveniles / Donald J. Black and Albert J. Reiss, Jr. -- The Kansas City preventive patrol experiment / George L. Kelling, Tony Pate, Duane Dieckman, and

	Charles E. Brown -- Florence Nightingale in pursuit of Willie Sutton: a theory of the police / Egon Bittner -- Broken windows: the police and neighborhood safety / James Q. Wilson and George L. Kelling -- The deterrent effects of arrest for domestic assault / Lawrence W. Sherman and Richard A. Berk -- Extent of unrecorded juvenile delinquency: tentative conclusions / James F. Short, Jr. and F. Ivan Nye -- Correlates of delinquency: the illusion of discrepancy between self-report and official measures / Michael J. Hindelang, Travis Hirschi, and Joseph G. Weis -- The American reformatory prison system / Zebulon Reed Brockway -- Discipline and punish / Michel Foucault -- Prisonization / Donald Clemmer -- The pains of imprisonment / Gresham M. Sykes -- The inmate social system / Gresham M. Sykes and Sheldon L. Messinger -- Society of women: a study of a women's prison / Rose Giallombardo -- Interpersonal dynamics in a simulated prison / Craig Haney, Curtis Banks, and Philip Zimbardo -- What works? Question and answers about prison reform / Robert Martinson -- Preventing crime: What works, what doesn't, what's promising / Lawrence W. Sherman, Denise C. Gottfredson, Doris L. MacKenzie, John Eck, Peter Reuter, and Shawn D. Bushway -- Frameworks of inquiry in the sociology of punishment / David Garland -- Extra-legal attributes and criminal sentencing: an assessment of a sociological viewpoint / John Hagan.
Subjects	Criminology--United States. Criminal justice, Administration of--United States.
Notes	Includes bibliographical references.

Containment in the community: supportive frameworks for thinking about antisocial behavior and mental health

LCCN	2011411179
Type of material	Book
Main title	Containment in the community: supportive frameworks for thinking about antisocial behavior and mental health / edited by Alla Rubitel and David Reiss.

Published/Created	London: Karnac, 2011.
Description	xxviii, 268 p.; 23 cm.
ISBN	9781855758483 1855758482
LC classification	RA790.55 .C63 2011
Related names	Rubitel, Alla. Reiss, David, 1937-
Subjects	Community mental health services. Antisocial Personality Disorder. Community Mental Health Services. Community mental health services. Gerichtliche Psychiatrie. Therapie. Dissoziale Persönlichkeitsstörung. Psychosoziale Versorgung. Täter. Psychische Gesundheit. Psychische Störung.
Notes	Includes bibliographical references and index.
Series	Portman papers series Portman papers.

Current directions in child psychopathology

LCCN	2009015755
Type of material	Book
Main title	Current directions in child psychopathology / edited by Kenneth A. Dodge.
Published/Created	Boston: Allyn & Bacon, c2010.
Description	vii, 188 p.: ill.; 23 cm.
ISBN	9780205680139 (pbk.) 0205680135 (pbk.)
LC classification	RJ499 .C87 2010
Related names	Dodge, Kenneth A.
Contents	Environmental factors that lead to child psychopathology -- Children's exposure to violence in the family and community -- Children's emotional security in the interparental relationship -- Beyond quality: parental and residential stability and children's adjustment -- Siblings' direct and indirect contributions

to child development -- How environments "get under the skin" to lead to psychopathology -- Maternal care and individual differences in defensive responses -- Corticotropin-releasing factor and the psychobiology of early-life stress -- Drug addiction during pregnancy: advances in maternal treatment and understanding child outcomes -- The role of prenatal maternal stress in child development -- Biological sensitivity to context -- Models of gene-environment interaction processes -- The interplay between genotypes and family relationships: reframing concepts of development and prevention -- Plasticity for affective neurocircuitry: how the environment affects gene expression -- For better and for worse: differential susceptibility to environmental influences -- From genes to brain to antisocial behavior -- Externalizing behavior disorders -- Identification of genes influencing a spectrum of externalizing psychopathology -- The role of neurobiological deficits in childhood antisocial behavior -- Violent children in developmental perspective: risk and protective factors and the mechanisms through which they (may) operate -- Risk taking in adolescence: new perspectives from brain and behavioral science -- School dropouts: prevention considerations, interventions, and challenges -- Neurodevelopmental disorders -- Evaluating the theory-of-mind hypothesis of autism -- Three reasons not to believe in an autism epidemic -- Neural mechanisms in dyslexia -- Learning abilities and disabilities: generalist genes, specialist environments.

Subjects Child psychopathology.

Notes "Pearson"--Spine.
Includes bibliographical references.

Series Readings from the Association for Psychological Science
Readings from the Association for Psychological Science.

Drug abuse and antisocial behavior.

LCCN	2016951435
Type of material	Book
Main title	Drug abuse and antisocial behavior.
Published/Produced	New York, NY: Springer Berlin Heidelberg, 2016.

Emotions, imagination, and moral reasoning

LCCN	2011036768
Type of material	Book
Main title	Emotions, imagination, and moral reasoning / editors, Robyn Langdon, Catriona Mackenzie.
Published/Created	New York, NY: Psychology Press, 2012.
Description	xiii, 366 p.: ill.; 24 cm.
ISBN	9781848729001 (hardcover: alk. paper)
LC classification	BF511 .E465 2012
Related names	Langdon, Robyn. Mackenzie, Catriona.
Contents	Introduction: philosophical and psychological perspectives on moral cognition / Robyn Langdon and Catriona Mackenzie -- The development of moral motivation at 6 years of age / Marc de Rosnay and Elian Fink -- Revisiting the role of empathy in childhood pathways to antisocial behavior / David J. Hawes and Mark R. Dadds -- Fiction, imagination, and ethics / Ian Ravenscroft -- Moral reasoning and psychopathic tendencies in the general community / Robyn Langdon and Kristy Delmas -- Strange moralities: vicarious emotion and moral emotions in machiavellian and psychopathic personality styles / Doris McIlwain, Jess Evans, Eleni Caldis, Fred Cicchini, Avi Aronstan, Adam Wright, and Alan Taylor -- The neurology of morality / Ricardo de Oliveira-Souza and Jorge Moll -- Cognitive enhancement and intuitive dualism: testing a possible link / Neil Levy and Jonathan McGuire -- Disgust and moral judgment / Trevor I. Case, Megan J. Oaten, and Richard J. Stevenson -- Thick concepts and their role in moral psychology / Chloë FitzGerald and Peter Goldie -- Emotions, reflection, and moral agency /

	Catriona Mackenzie -- Living with one's choices: moral reasoning in vitro and in vivo / Jeanette Kennett -- Are intentionality judgments fundamentally moral? / Bertram F. Malle and Steve Guglielmo -- Coreactive attitudes and the making of moral community / Victoria McGeer -- Reflections on emotions, imagination, and moral reasoning: toward an integrated, multidisciplinary approach to moral cognition / Wayne Christensen and John Sutton.
Subjects	Emotions. Imagination. Reasoning. Cognitive psychology.
Notes	Includes bibliographical references and index.
Series	Macquarie monographs in cognitive science

Enhancing student learning in middle school

LCCN	2010013879
Type of material	Book
Personal name	Casas, Martha.
Main title	Enhancing student learning in middle school / Martha Casas.
Published/Created	New York, NY: Routledge, 2011.
Description	xvi, 361 p.: ill.; 26 cm.
ISBN	9780415801768 (hardback: alk. paper) 9780415801775 (pbk.: alk. paper) 9780203847107 (e-book)
LC classification	LB1623 .C37 2011
Contents	Rationalizing the middle school concept -- Theoretical frameworks -- Motivational theories and early adolescence -- Effective classroom management -- What is antisocial behavior? -- Designing and enacting the curriculum -- Using multicultural education to enhance student engagement in learning -- Assessing student learning.
Subjects	Middle school teaching. Middle school education.
Notes	Includes bibliographical references (p. [319]-336) and index.

Evidence-based psychotherapies for children and adolescents

LCCN	2009049689
Type of material	Book
Main title	Evidence-based psychotherapies for children and adolescents / edited by John R. Weisz, Alan E. Kazdin.
Edition	2nd ed.
Published/Created	New York: Guilford Press, c2010.
Description	xx, 602 p.: ill.; 26 cm.
ISBN	9781593859749 (hardcover: alk. paper) 1593859740 (hardcover: alk. paper)
LC classification	RJ504 .E95 2010
Related names	Weisz, John R. Kazdin, Alan E.
Contents	Introduction: context, background, and goals / Alan E. Kazdin and John R. Weisz -- Ethical issues in child and adolescent psychosocial treatment research / Kimberly Eaton Hoagwood and Mary A. Cavaleri -- Developmental issues and considerations in research and practice / Grayson N. Holmbeck, Katie A. Devine, and Elizabeth F. Bruno -- Child-focused treatment of anxiety / Philip C. Kendall, Jami M. Furr, and Jennifer L. Podell -- Interventions for anxiety disorders in children using group cognitive-behavioral therapy with family involvement / Kristine M. Pahl and Paula M. Barrett -- Treating pediatric obsessive-compulsive disorder using exposure-based cognitive-behavioral therapy / Martin E. Franklin, Jennifer Freeman, and John S. March -- Cognitive-behavioral therapy for depression: the ACTION treatment program for girls / Kevin D. Stark ... [et al.] -- Group cognitive-behavioral treatment for adolescent depression / Gregory N. Clarke and Lynn L. DeBar -- Treating depression in adolescents using individual cognitive-behavioral therapy / V. Robin Weersing and David A. Brent -- Treating adolescent depression using interpersonal psychotherapy / Colleen M. Jacobson and Laura Mufson -- Parent management training-Oregon model: an intervention for antisocial behavior in children and adolescents / Marion S. Forgatch and Gerald R.

Patterson -- Parent-child interaction therapy and the treatment of disruptive behavior disorders / Alison Zisser and Sheila M. Eyberg -- The incredible years parents, teachers, and children training series: a multifaceted treatment approach for young children with conduct disorders / Carolyn Webster-Stratton and M. Jamila Reid -- Problem-solving skills training and parent management training for oppositional defiant disorders and conduct disorder / Alan E. Kazdin -- Anger control training for aggressive youths / John E. Lochman ... [et al.] -- Multidimensional treatment foster care for adolescents: processes and outcomes / Dana K. Smith and Patricia Chamberlain -- Treating serious antisocial behavior using multisystemic therapy / Scott W. Henggeler and Cindy Schaeffer -- Summer treatment programs for attention-deficit/hyperactivity disorder / William E. Pelham, Jr. ... [et al.] -- Trauma-focused cognitive-behavioral therapy for traumatized children / Judith A. Cohen, Anthony P. Mannarino, and Esther Deblinger -- Early and intensive behavioral intervention in autism / Tristram Smith -- Empirically supported pivotal response treatment for children with autism spectrum disorders / Robert L. Koegel ... [et al.] -- Family therapy for adolescents with anorexia nervosa / Arthur L. Robin and Daniel le Grange -- Behavioral treatment for enuresis / Arthur C. Houts -- Treating Hispanic youths using brief strategic family therapy / Michael S. Robbins ... [et al.] -- Treating Hispanic children and adolescents using narrative therapy / Robert G. Malgady -- Functional family therapy for adolescent substance use disorders / Holly Barrett Waldron and Janet L. Brody -- Treating adolescent substance abuse using multidimensional family therapy / Howard A. Liddle -- Implementation of evidence-based treatments for children and adolescents: research findings and their implications for the future / Dean L. Fixsen ... [et al.] -- Assessing the effects of evidence-based psychotherapies with ethnic minority youths / Stanley

	J. Huey, Jr. and Antonio J. Polo -- Adapting cognitive-behavioral therapy for depression to fit diverse youths and contexts: applying the deployment-focused model of treatment development and testing / Sarah Kate Bearman ... [et al.] -- Building evidence-based systems in children's mental health / Bruce F. Chorpita and Eric L. Daleiden -- Nationwide dissemination of effective parenting interventions: building a parenting academy for England / Stephen Scott -- The international dissemination of the triple P-Positive Parenting Program / Matthew R. Sanders and Majella Murphy-Brennan -- From policy pinball to purposeful partnership: the policy contexts of multisystemic therapy transport and dissemination / Sonja K. Schoenwald -- The present and future of evidence-based psychotherapies for children and adolescents / John R. Weisz and Alan E. Kazdin.
Subjects	Child psychotherapy. Adolescent psychotherapy. Evidence-based psychiatry. Psychotherapy. Adolescent. Child. Evidence-Based Medicine.
Notes	Includes bibliographical references and indexes.

Handbook of adult psychopathology in Asians: theory, diagnosis, and treatment

LCCN	2011031966
Type of material	Book
Main title	Handbook of adult psychopathology in Asians: theory, diagnosis, and treatment / edited by Edward C. Chang.
Published/Created	Oxford; New York: Oxford University Press, c2012.
Description	xvii, 467 p.: ill.; 26 cm.
ISBN	9780195179064 (alk. paper) 0195179064 (alk. paper)
LC classification	RC451.A72 H36 2012
Related names	Chang, Edward C. (Edward Chin-Ho)
Contents	Introduction to the handbook: from nomothetic to

	idiographic approaches -- Edward C. Chang and Cathryn G. Fabian -- What is the psychology of Asians? / Anne Saw and Sumie Okazaki -- Issues in the research and assessment of psychopathology in Asians -- Phillip D. Akutsu and Joyce P. Chu -- Substance use disorders in Asians / Eunice C. Wong and Karen Chan Osilla -- Schizophrenia and other psychosis in Asians and Asian Americans -- Keh-Ming Lin, Hai-Gwo Hwu, and Ming T. Tsuang -- Mood disorders in Asians / Albert Yeung and Doris Chang -- Anxiety disorders in Asians / Janie J. Hong -- Somatoform disorders in Asians / Winnie W.S. Mak, Fanny M. Cheung, and Freedom Leung -- Dissociation, conversion, and possession disorder in Asians -- Wen-Shing Tseng and Cong Zhong -- Antisocial behavior and externalizing disorders among Asians, Asian Americans, and Pacific Islander populations -- Sopagna Eap Braje ... [et al.] -- Eating disorders in Asians / Lillian Huang Cummins, Janice Delgado Lehman, and Rebecca Chun Liu -- Sleep disorders in Asians / Donald M. Sesso, Allison V. Chan, and Clete A. Kushida -- Adjustment disorders in Asians / Kevin M. Chun and Jeanette Hsu -- Personality disorders in Asians / Andrew G. Ryder ... [et al.] -- Culture-related specific psychiatric syndromes observed in Asia -- Wen-Shing Tseng ... [et al.]-- Unique psychotherapies developed in Asia / Wen-Shing Tseng ... [et. al.] -- Where do we go from here?: future directions, challenges, and considerations / Cathryn G. Fabian and Edward C. Chang .
Subjects	Mental illness--Asia. Psychotherapy--Asia. Asian Continental Ancestry Group--psychology--Asia. Mental Disorders--ethnology--Asia.
Notes	Includes bibliographical references.

Handbook of child and adolescent psychopathy

LCCN	2009051596
Type of material	Book

Main title	Handbook of child and adolescent psychopathy / edited by Randall T. Salekin, Donald R. Lynam.
Published/Created	New York: Guilford Press, c2010.
Description	xi, 451 p.: ill.; 24 cm.
ISBN	9781606236826 (hardcover: acid-free paper) 1606236822 (hardcover: acid-free paper)
LC classification	RJ499.3 .H263 2010
Related names	Salekin, Randall T. Lynam, Donald R.
Contents	Child and adolescent psychopathy: an introduction / Randall T. Salekin and Donald R. Lynam -- Conceptualizing the psychopathic personality: disinhibited, bold,-- or just plain mean? / Christopher J. Patrick -- Historical conceptions of risk subtyping among children and adolescents / John E. Lochman ... [et al.] -- Assessment of child and adolescent psychopathy / Julie S. Kotler and Robert J. McMahon -- Genetics of child and adolescent psychopathy / Essi Viding and Henrik Larsson -- Callous-unemotional traits and their importance to causal models of severe antisocial behavior in youth / Stuart F. White and Paul J. Frick -- A cognitive neuroscience perspective on child and adolescent psychopathy / R. James, R. Blair -- Child and adolescent psychopathy and personality / Donald R. Lynam -- Environmental influences on child and adolescent psychopathy / David P. Farrington, Simone Ullrich, and Randall T. Salekin -- Stability and change of psychopathic traits: what do we know? / Henrik Andershed -- Psychopathic traits in children and adolescents: the relationship with antisocial behaviors and aggression / Adelle E. Forth and Angela S. Book -- Relationships of child and adolescent psychopathy to other forms of psychopathology / Kathrin Sevecke and David S. Kosson -- The influences of gender and culture on child and adolescent psychopathy / Edelyn Verona, Naomi Sadeh, and Shabnam Javdani -- Treatment of child and adolescent psychopathy: focusing on change / Randall T. Salekin -- Forensic issues for child and adolescent

	psychopathy / Michael J. Vitacco, Randall T. Salekin, and Richard Rogers -- Child and adolescent psychopathy: the road ahead / Randall T. Salekin and Donald R. Lynam.
Subjects	Child psychopathology--Handbooks, manuals, etc. Antisocial Personality Disorder. Adolescent. Child.
Notes	Includes bibliographical references and indexes.

How are online activities affecting society?

LCCN	2013017164
Type of material	Book
Personal name	Szumski, Bonnie, 1958-
Main title	How are online activities affecting society? / Bonnie Szumski and Jill Karson (INCONTROVERSY).
Published/Produced	San Diego, CA: Reference Point Press, [2014].
Description	96 pages: color illustrations; 24 cm.
ISBN	9781601525468 (hardback) 160152546X (hardback)
LC classification	HM742 .S98 2014
Related names	Karson, Jill.
Contents	What is the origin of the debate about the societal effects of online activities? -- How do online activities affect youth? -- Are online activities addictive? -- Do online activities promote antisocial behavior? -- How do online activities impact political and world events?.
Subjects	Online social networks--Juvenile literature. Internet--History--Juvenile literature.
Notes	Includes bibliographical references and index. Grade 9 to 12
Series	In controversy

Juvenile justice and delinquency

LCCN	2010000205
Type of material	Book
Main title	Juvenile justice and delinquency / David W. Springer, editor; Albert R. Roberts, editor.
Published/Created	Sudbury, Mass.: Jones and Bartlett Publishers, c2011.

Description	xxix, 492 p.: ill.; 23 cm.
ISBN	9780763760564 0763760560
LC classification	HV9104 .J88 2011
Related names	Springer, David W. Roberts, Albert R.
Contents	A brief historical overview of juvenile justice and juvenile delinquency -- Trends in American youth crime -- Scaling up from juvenile court records to offenses committed -- Reforming juvenile justice through comprehensive community planning -- Early intervention of delinquency and later criminal offending -- Effectiveness of early crime prevention -- From risk identification to risk management: a comprehensive strategy for young children engaging in antisocial behavior -- The power of education in juvenile justice -- Effective programs to reduce school bullying -- Theories of delinquency -- Developmental pathways and life trajectories of delinquency -- Family influences on delinquency -- The late modern world of adolescence and sociological theories of delinquency -- Juvenile justice treatment and policy alternatives -- Screening and assessment of mental health disorders and risk of re-offending among juvenile offenders -- Youth suicide in juvenile justice settings: prevention through empirically based assessment and crisis intervention -- Police responses to criminal and juvenile justice in the 21st century -- State-of-the-art juvenile detention: in search of a new normal -- Therapeutic jurisprudence and juvenile court -- Innovative justice for youth with mental health and substance use disorders: juvenile drug and mental health courts.
Subjects	Juvenile justice, Administration of--United States. Juvenile delinquency--United States.
Notes	Includes bibliographical references and index.

Loaded: money, psychology, and how to get ahead without leaving your values behind

LCCN	2016001707
Type of material	Book
Personal name	Newcomb, Sarah C., author.
Main title	Loaded: money, psychology, and how to get ahead without leaving your values behind / Sarah Newcomb, PhD.
Published/Produced	Hoboken, New Jersey: John Wiley & Sons, Inc., [2016]
ISBN	978-1-11925-832-2 (hardback)
LC classification	HG179 .N447 2016
Summary	"Research studies over the past few decades reveal an interesting paradox: Lack of money is linked to depression, relationship problems, lower performance on difficult tasks, and even shorter life expectancy, yet just thinking about money can lead to antisocial behavior and reduce compassion. It would appear that money creates a lose-lose scenario: If you don't have it, your performance suffers, your relationships suffer, and you may die sooner. But, if you have great wealth, you may be more likely to engage in victim blaming, and less likely to help others by choice. How do we solve this conflict? Do we have to choose between caring about people and caring about money? How do we create lives of great value, without compromising our own deep values? We do it by working with our psychology. By mindfully developing a healthy relationship with money and learning some simple new ways of thinking, we can avoid the psychological dangers that can accompany both poverty and wealth"-- Provided by publisher. "A majority (62%) of American adults are losing sleep over their finances, leading to stress-related health problems and lower life satisfaction. The common phrase, "Money is the root of all evil," exposes a deep cultural distrust for money itself, as if currency has the power to corrupt otherwise good people. The belief that money is a necessary but corrupting force is

sprinkled heavily throughout our cultural stories and public conversations. Feelings of personal desperation combined with negative beliefs about wealth can lead to a complex emotional relationship with money. Financial psychologists have observed for decades that the way that we think and feel about money has a powerful effect on how we handle -- or mishandle -- this resource in our own lives. It takes more than financial advice to reach people who have a difficult relationship with money. It takes understanding and a validation of their experience and perspective. This book approaches money management from a fresh angle, beginning with the recognition that our experiences with money can often run counter to our core values. Deeply researched, yet written in an approachable, conversational tone, this book offers insight into how the reader's personal experiences have shaped their financial attitudes, and how they can have a healthier relationship with their own money. The book will first examine the roots and consequences of core money beliefs and then use a unique and personalized Values-Based approach to budgeting and money management. Worksheets and personal money psychology assessments supplement the text. "--Provided by publisher.

Contents Machine generated contents note: Preface Acknowledgments Chapter 1 Introduction: When it comes to money, we've all got issues Chapter 2 Money Messages We Don't Talk About Money We Talk About Money Constantly From Freud to Frodo: The stories we tell each other Kathy's Story The Stories We Tell Ourselves Stories can help or Hurt Heuristics and Biases Shape Our Stories Identifying Core Beliefs Challenging Core Beliefs Using Science to Our Advantage Chapter 3 Poverty, Privilege, and Prejudice: A crash course in the science of money psychology Money and Social Psychology: How poverty, privilege, and comparisons affect our minds and behavior Money and Cognitive Psychology: How

	specific thinking patterns affect financial decisions Making Change Chapter 4 The LOADED Budget: Creating a human-centered money management plan What's Wrong With Your Budget? Where Does Your Money Come From? Assets and Resources Where Does Your Money Go? Putting it All Together: MEconomics The Power of Perspective Keeping Yourself on Track Enjoying a Loaded Life: Living in harmony with your money and your values APPENDIX A: Self-Assessments 1. Write Your Personal Financial Narrative 2. Define Your Core Beliefs 3. Financial Management & Behaviors Scale 4. Emotions and Money 5. Mental Imagery 6. Behavior Identification Form 7. How Impulsive Are You? 8. Big 5 Financial Literacy Questions APPENDIX B: Exercises & Worksheets 1. Change the narrative 2. Find a counter-example 3. Age-progression 4. Future Visualization Exercises 5. Exercises to Combat MoneyThink 6. Affirm core values 7. Cash Flow Sheet 8. Resources Worksheet 9. Needs Worksheet 10. Your Meconomy About the Author Index.
Subjects	Finance, Personal--Psychological aspects. Economics--Psychological aspects. Business & Economics / Personal Finance / Money Management. Business & Economics / Personal Finance / General. Business & Economics / Personal Finance / Investing.
Notes	Includes index.
Additional formats	Online version: Newcomb, Sarah C., author. Loaded Hoboken, New Jersey: John Wiley & Sons, Inc., [2016] 9781119258339 (DLC) 2016010034

Measuring crime & criminality

LCCN	2011410638
Type of material	Book
Main title	Measuring crime & criminality / John MacDonald, editor.
Published/Created	New Brunswick, NJ: Transaction Publishers, c2011.
Description	xvi, 387 p.: ill.; 23 cm.

ISBN	9781412814812 (hbk.) 1412814812 (hbk.)
LC classification	HV6024.5 .M44 2011
Variant title	Measuring crime and criminality
Related names	MacDonald, John M. (John Michael), 1972-
Summary	"Measuring Crime and Criminality focuses on how different approaches to measuring crime and criminality are used to test existing criminological theories. Each chapter reviews a key approach for measuring criminal behavior and discusses its strengths or weaknesses for explaining the facts of crime or answers to central issues of criminological inquiry. The book describes the state of the field on different approaches for measuring crime and criminality as seen by prominent scholars in the field. Among the featured contributions are: The Use of Official Reports and Victimization Data for Testing Criminological Theories; The Design and Analysis of Experiments in Criminology; and Growth Curve/Mixture Models for Measuring Criminal Careers. Also included are papers titled: Counterfactual Methods of Causal Inference and Their Application to Criminology; Measuring Gene-Environment Interactions in the Cause of Antisocial Behavior and What Has Been Gained and Lost through Longitudinal Research and Advanced Statistical Models? This volume of Advances in Criminological Theory illustrates how understanding the various ways criminal behavior is measured is useful for developing theoretical insights on the causes of crime."--Publisher's website.
Contents	Introduction: the measurement of crime and estimating treatment effects in criminology / John M. MacDonald -- The self-report method and the development of criminological theory / Terence P. Thornberry and Marvin D. Krohn -- Socially desirable response bias in criminology: an example of its effect in testing the effects of self-control / John M. MacDonald, Andrew Morral, and Alex R. Piquero -- How do we measure

	the severity of crimes? New estimates of the cost of criminal victimization / John K. Roman -- Communities and crime theories: construct validation deficits, a paucity of comparisons, and a Boudon-Coleman metamodel resolution / Ralph B. Taylor -- The coming of a networked criminology? / Andrew V. Papachristos -- What can genetically informed research tell us about the causes of crime? / Candice L. Odgers and Michael A. Russell -- Bounding disagreements about treatment effects with an application to criminology / Charles F. Manski and Daniel S. Nagin -- Randomized experiments and the advancement of criminological theory / Geoffrey C. Barnes and Jordan M. Hyatt -- Causal interference via natural experiments and instrumental variables: the effect of "knifing off" from the past / David S. Kirk -- Criminal career research: a statistical and substantive comparison of growth modeling approaches / Christopher J. Sullivan and Alex R. Piquero -- Understanding desistance: theory testing with formal empirical models / Shawn D. Bushway and Raymond Paternoster -- Meta-analysis and the relative support for various criminological theories / Ojmarrh Mitchell.
Subjects	Criminology--Research. Criminal behavior.
Notes	Includes bibliographical references and index.
Series	Advances in criminological theory; v. 17

Multimethod clinical assessment

LCCN	2014011934
Type of material	Book
Main title	Multimethod clinical assessment / edited by Christopher J. Hopwood, Robert F. Bornstein.
Published/Produced	New York: The Guilford Press, [2014].
Description	xii, 476 pages: illustrations; 24 cm
ISBN	9781462516018 (hardback: acid-free paper)
LC classification	BF698.5 .M85 2014
Related names	Hopwood, Christopher J., 1976- editor of compilation. Bornstein, Robert F., editor of compilation.

Summary	"From leading authorities, this book presents evidence-based strategies for using multimethod assessment to enhance clinical practice. The volume is organized around key assessment targets in the areas of personality, psychopathology, and clinical management (for example, treatment planning and progress monitoring). Each chapter presents multiple methods that are particularly useful for assessing the issue at hand, provides a framework for using these methods together, and reviews the empirical data supporting their integration. Illustrative case examples clarify the approaches described and show how incorporating assessment into treatment can strengthen the therapeutic relationship. Subject Areas/Keywords: assessments, case formulation, clinical evaluation, diagnosis, disorders, interviewing, multimethod, personality, psychodynamic, psychological testing, psychopathology, psychotherapy, tests, therapists, treatment planning Audience: Practitioners and students in clinical psychology; also of interest to psychiatrists, social workers, and other evaluators in clinical and forensic settings"-- Provided by publisher.
Contents	Machine generated contents note: Introduction to Multimethod Clinical Assessment, Robert F. Bornstein and Christopher J. Hopwood -- I. Personality and Individual Differences -- 1. Multimethod Clinical Assessment of Traits, Janine Galione and Thomas F. Oltmanns -- 2. Multimethod Clinical Assessment of Interpersonal Dynamics, Aaron L. Pincus, Pamela Sadler, Erik Woody, Michael J. Roche, Katherine M. Thomas, and Aidan G. C. Wright -- 3. Multimethod Assessment of Affective Processes, Rachel L. Tomko and Timothy J. Trull -- 4. Multimethod Assessment of Existential Concerns: A Terror Management Perspective, Spee Kosloff, Molly Maxfield, and Sheldon Solomon -- 5. Mulitmethod Assessment of Implicit and Explicit Processes, Alex Cogswell and Natalie Emmert -- II. Psychopathology and Resilience -- 6. Multimethod Assessment of Anxiety: Integrating

Data from Subjective Experience, Cognitive Performance, and Neurophysiological Measures, Jason S. Moser, Amy Przeworski, Hans S. Schroder, and Kimberly Marie Dunbeck -- 7. Multimethod Assessment of the Adult Externalizing Spectrum: Disorders of Antisocial Behavior and Substance Abuse, Daniel M. Blonigen and Amy Wytiaz -- 8. Clinical Assessment of Thought Quality: A Multimethod Approach, Mark A. Blais and Iruma Bello -- 9. Multimethod Assessment of Resilience: Integration with an Individual-Differences Model, Christy A. Denckla and Anthony D. Mancini -- III. Clinical Management -- 10. Multimethod Assessment and Treatment Planning, Joni L. Mihura and Robert A. Graceffo -- 11. Psychotherapy Progress and Process Assessment, A. Pascual-Leone, Terence Singh, Shawn Harrington, and Nikita Yeryomenko -- 12. Multimethod Assessment of Distortion: Integrating Data from Interviews, Collateral Records, and Standardized Assessment Tools, Danielle Burchett and R. Michael Bagby -- 13. Multimethod Risk Assessment, Michael L. Stanfill, Suzanne O'Brien, and Donald J. Viglione, Jr. -- 14. Integration and Therapeutic Presentation of Multimethod Assessment Results: An Empirically Supported Framework and Case Example, Justin D. Smith and Stephen E. Finn -- Conclusion: Toward a Framework for Integrating Multimethod Clinical Assessment Data, Christopher J. Hopwood and Robert F. Bornstein.

Subjects Psychoanalysis.
Personality assessment.
Psychology / Clinical Psychology.
Medical / Psychiatry / General.
Psychology / Assessment, Testing & Measurement.
Medical / Nursing / Mental Health.

Notes Includes bibliographical references and indexes.

Narcissism and Machiavellianism in youth: implications for the development of adaptive and maladaptive behavior

LCCN	2010004967
Type of material	Book
Main title	Narcissism and Machiavellianism in youth: implications for the development of adaptive and maladaptive behavior / edited by Christopher T. Barry ... [et al.].
Edition	1st ed.
Published/Created	Washington, DC: American Psychological Association, c2011.
Description	xi, 282 p.: ill.; 26 cm.
ISBN	9781433808456 1433808455
LC classification	BF575.N35 N357 2011
Related names	Barry, Christopher T.
Contents	Emerging personality in childhood and adolescence: implications for the development of narcissism and Machiavellianism / Jennifer L. Tackett and Sarah Mackrell -- Psychopathy, narcissism, and Machiavellianism: distinct yet intertwining personality constructs / Kurt K. Stellwagen -- Self-esteem, narcissism, and Machiavellianism: implications for understanding antisocial behavior in adolescents and young adults / Edward A. Witt, M. Brent Donnellan, and Kali H. Trzesniewski -- Developmental and theoretical influences on the conceptualization and assessment of youth narcissism / Christopher T. Barry, Marion T. Wallace, and Matthew D. Guelker -- Adaptive and maladaptive narcissism in adolescent development / Patrick L. Hill and Daniel K. Lapsley -- Defensive egotism and aggression in childhood: a new lens on the self-esteem paradox / Marlene Sandstrom -- On environmental sources of child narcissism: are parents really to blame? / Robert S. Horton -- Moving beyond parents in the etiology of narcissistic traits / Jason J. Washburn and Leah D. Paskar -- Narcissism, positive illusory bias, and externalizing behaviors / Tammy D. Barry ... [et al.] -- Early adoption of

	Machiavellian attitudes: implications for children's interpersonal relationships / Virginia Slaughter -- The new scoundrel on the schoolyard: contributions of Machiavellianism to the understanding of youth aggression / Patricia K. Kerig and Holli E. Sink -- Young Machiavellians and the traces of shame: coping with vulnerability to a toxic affect / Doris McIlwain -- Machiavellianism in elementary school children: risk and adaptation / Hanneke Palmen ... [et al.].
Subjects	Narcissism. Machiavellianism (Psychology)
Notes	Includes bibliographical references and index.

Neuroimaging genetics: principles and practices

LCCN	2015012030
Type of material	Book
Main title	Neuroimaging genetics: principles and practices / edited by Kristin L. Bigos, Ahmad R. Hariri, Daniel R. Weinberger.
Published/Produced	Oxford; New York: Oxford University Press, [2016]
ISBN	9780199920211
LC classification	QP376.6
Related names	Bigos, Kristin L., editor. Hariri, Ahmad R., 1972- , editor. Weinberger, Daniel R. (Daniel Roy)
Contents	Imaging genetics / Kristin L. Bigos, Ahmad R. Hariri, Daniel R. Weinberger -- Molecular neuroimaging genetics / Patrick M. Fisher and Gitte M. Knudsen -- Neuroreceptor imaging of genetic variation impacting the serotonin transporter / Greg Perlman, Christine DeLorenzo, J. John Mann, Ramin Parsey -- Imaging of genetic variation impacting dopamine transmission parameters / Elsmarieke van de Giessen, Rassil Ghazzaoui, Raj Narendran, Anissa Abi-Dargham -- Imaging genetics of dopamine synaptic terminal activity / Giuseppe Blasi and Alessandro Bertolino -- Variability of antidepressant drug response: contribution of imaging genetics studies / Ulrich Rabl, Bernhard M. Meyer, Lukas Pezawas -- Imaging

genetics of pharmacological response in psychiatric disorders / Philip R. Szeszko and Anil K. Malhotra -- Imaging genetics of Williams syndrome / Daniel P. Eisenberg, Ranjani Prabhakaran, Karen F. Berman -- Identifying unanticipated genes and mechanisms in serious mental illness: GWAS based imaging genetics strategies / Steven G. Potkin, Theo G. M. van Erp, Shichun Ling, Fabio Macciardi, Xiaohui Xie -- Imaging genetics of brain structure / Jason L. Stein, Derrek P. Hibar, Paul M. Thompson -- Imaging genetics of the reward system / Caroline F. Zink -- Imaging genetics of schizophrenia / Thomas M. Lancaster, Joanne Doherty, David E. J. Linden, Jeremy Hall -- Imaging genetics of depression / Matthew D. Sacchet, Lara C. Foland-Ross, Ian H. Gotlib -- Imaging genetics of anxiety disorders / Mats Fredrikson -- Imaging genetics of bipolar disorder / Ole A. Andreassen -- Genetic-neuroimaging studies of basal ganglia disorders / Trevor W. Robbins, James B. Rowe, Roger A. Barker -- Imaging genetics of antisocial behavior and psychopathy / Hayley M. Dorfman, Joshua W. Buckholtz -- Incorporating the environment into neurogenetics research an imaging gene by environment interactions (IG x E) approach / Luke Hyde, Ryan Bogdan, Ahmad R. Hariri -- Imaging genetics of episodic memory / Björn Rasch, Susanne Erk, Andreas Papassotiropoulos, Dominique J.-F. de Quervain -- Imaging genetics of working memory / Tristram A. Lett, Eva J. Brandl, Daniel J. Müller, Andreas Heinz, Henrik Walter -- Neurobiology and genetics of cognitive aging: insights from neuroimaging studies / John C. Muse, Milap Nowrangi, Daniel R. Weinberger, Venkata S. Mattay -- Neuroimaging genetics of Alzheimer's disease / Theresa M. Harrison, Alison C. Burggren, Susan Y. Bookheimer -- Imaging genetics of the hypothalamic pituitary adrenal axis: implications for psychopathology / Nadia S. Corral-Frias, Lindsay J. Michalski, Christina R. Di Iorio, Ryan Bogdan.

Subjects	Neuroimaging. Brain--physiology. Brain Chemistry--genetics. Mental Disorders--genetics.
Notes	Includes bibliographical references and index.

Neuroscience for the mental health clinician

LCCN	2016001914
Type of material	Book
Personal name	Pliszka, Steven R., author.
Main title	Neuroscience for the mental health clinician / Steven R. Pliszka.
Edition	Second edition.
Published/Produced	New York: The Guilford Press, [2016]
ISBN	9781462527113 (paperback) 9781462527120 (hardcover)
LC classification	RC341 .P58 2016
Contents	I. Basic: Introduction -- Draw the brain: introduction to clinical neuroanatomy -- Neuronal communication -- Neurotransmitters -- Genetics and epigenetics -- Fear, reward, and action -- Attention and memory -- Higher cognitive functioning -- II. Mental disorders: Attention-deficit/hyperactivity disorder -- Aggression, antisocial behavior, and substance abuse -- Mood and anxiety disorders -- Schizophrenia -- Autism spectrum disorders -- Dementia.
Subjects	Neurosciences.
Notes	Includes bibliographical references and index.

Principles of psychiatric genetics

LCCN	2012000081
Type of material	Book
Main title	Principles of psychiatric genetics / edited by John I. Nurnberger Jr., Wade H. Berrettini.
Published/Created	Cambridge; New York: Cambridge University Press, 2012.
Description	xii, 402 p.: col. ill.; 26 cm.
ISBN	9780521896498 (hardback)
LC classification	RC455.4.G4 P75 2012

Related names	Nurnberger, John I., 1946- Berrettini, Wade.
Summary	"Disorders of behavior represent some of the most common and disabling diseases affecting humankind; however, despite their worldwide distribution, genetic influences on these illnesses are often overlooked by families and mental health professionals. Psychiatric genetics is a rapidly advancing field, elucidating the varied roles of specific genes and their interactions in brain development and dysregulation. Principles of Psychiatric Genetics includes 22 disorder-based chapters covering, amongst other conditions, schizophrenia, mood disorders, anxiety disorders, Alzheimer's disease, learning and developmental disorders, eating disorders and personality disorders. Supporting chapters focus on issues of genetic epidemiology, molecular and statistical methods, pharmacogenetics, epigenetics, gene expression studies, online genetic databases and ethical issues. Written by an international team of contributors, and fully updated with the latest results from genome-wide association studies, this comprehensive text is an indispensable reference for psychiatrists, neurologists, psychologists and anyone involved in psychiatric genetic studies"--Provided by publisher.
Contents	Machine generated contents note: Preface; 1. Contribution of genetic epidemiology to our understanding of psychiatric disorders Kathleen Reis Merikangas and Anibal Cravchik; 2. A basic overview of contemporary human genetic analysis strategies Ondrej Libiger and Nicholas J. Schork; 3. In silico analysis strategies and resources for psychiatric genetics research Ali Torkamani, Trygve Bakken and Nicholas J. Schork; 4. Gene expression studies in psychiatric disorders Alexander B. Niculescu; 5. Pharmacogenetics in psychiatry Falk W. Lohoff; 6. Functional validation of candidate genetic susceptibility factors for major mental illnesses: from protein chemistry, cell biology, animal study, to

human brain imaging Akira Sawa, Wanli W. Smith, Saurav Seshadri, Akiko Hayashi-Takagi, Hanna Jaaro-Peled and Atsushi Kamiya; 7. Epigenetic mechanisms in drug addiction and depression William Renthal and Eric J. Nestler; 8. Panic disorder Ardesheer Talati and Myrna M. Weissman; 9. The genetics of phobic disorders and generalized anxiety disorder Raymond R. Crowe; 10. Genetic contributions to obsessive-compulsive disorder (OCD) and OCD-related disorders Dennis L. Murphy, Pablo R. Moya, Jens R. Wendland and Kiara Timpano; 11. Post-traumatic stress disorder Michael J. Lyons, Tyler Zink and Karestan C. Koenen; 12. Antisocial behavior: gene environment interplay Laura A. Baker, Catherine Tuvblad, Serena Bedzjian and Adrian Raine; 13. Learning disabilities Shelley D. Smith; 14. Autism and autism spectrum disorders Daniel H. Geschwind and Maricela Alarcon; 15. Genetics of major depression James B. Potash; 16. The genetics of anorexia and bulimia nervosa Andrew W. Bergen, Jennifer Wessel and Walter H. Kaye; 17. Genetics and common human obesity R. Arlen Price; 18. Alcoholism Howard J. Edenberg; 19. Nicotine dependence Sarah Hartz and Laura Bierut; 20. Genetics of stimulant dependence Joseph F. Cubells and Yi-Lang Tang; 21. Genetics of personality disorders C. Robert Cloninger; 22. Ethical issues in behavioral genetics Stephen H. Dinwiddie, Jinger Hoop and Elliot Gershon; 23. Genetics of Tourette syndrome and related disorders Maria G. Motlagh, Thomas V. Fernandez and James F. Leckman; 24. Endophenotypes Bernice Porjesz; 25. Developmental disorders Craig A. Erickson, Khendra I. Peay and Christopher J. McDougle; Index.

Subjects	Mental Disorders--genetics. Mental Disorders--epidemiology.

Social psychology: new developments

LCCN	2012005455
Type of material	Book

Main title	Social psychology: new developments / Jan M. Turner and Andrew D. Mitchell.
Published/Created	Hauppauge, NY: Nova Science Publishers, c2012.
Description	xi, 149 p.; 24 cm.
ISBN	9781620811429 (hardcover)
LC classification	HM1033 .S638 2012
Related names	Turner, Jan M. Mitchell, Andrew D.
Contents	Preface -- Cultural, social, and gender influences on casual sex: new developments / Elaine Hatfield, Elisabeth Sarah Steele Hutchison, Lisamarie Bensman, Danielle M. Young, Richard L. Rapson, and others -- Psychological assessment in a new key: allostatic load (stress age) and resilience / Thomas G. Arizmendi -- Emerging forms of identity online: opportunities for extending theorising about identity through textual analysis / Natilene Bowker -- Anger, defense mechanisms, and integrative self-knowledge in Iranian coronary heart disease and cancer patients / Nima Ghorbani, Sahar Tahbaz, P.J. Watson, Zhuo Chen, and others -- A further examination of the relationships among peer victimization, physical activity, and social psychological adjustment in obese youth / Charisse Williams, Eric A. Storch, Marilynn Paradora -- Antisocial behavior in children with ADHD: causes and treatment / Efrosini Kalyva -- Index.
Subjects	Social psychology.
Notes	Includes index.
Series	Psychology of emotions, motivations and actions

The development of criminal and antisocial behavior

LCCN	2014954233
Type of material	Book
Personal name	Morizot, Julien.
Main title	The development of criminal and antisocial behavior / Julien Morizot.
Published/Produced	New York: Springer, 2014.
Links	Contributor biographical information http://www.loc.gov/catdir/enhancements/fy1504/2014954233-b.html

	Publisher description http://www.loc.gov/catdir/enhancements/fy1504/2014954233-d.html Table of contents only http://www.loc.gov/catdir/enhancements/fy1504/2014954233-t.html
ISBN	9783319087191

The Handbook of forensic psychopathology and treatment

LCCN	2015045846
Type of material	Book
Main title	The Handbook of forensic psychopathology and treatment / edited by Maaike Cima.
Published/Produced	London; New York: Routledge/taylor & Francis Group, 2016.
Description	xii, 390 pages; 24 cm
ISBN	9780415657747 (hardback) 9780415657754 (pbk.)
LC classification	RA1151 .H246 2016
Related names	Cima-Knijff, Maaike José, 1973- , editor.
Contents	Defining forensic psycho(patho)logy -- Scientific research in forensic samples development of antisocial behavior -- Children at risk for serious conduct problems -- Biological approaches to externalizing disorders and juvenile psychopathic traits -- Juvenile offenders -- Conscience: moral cognitions, moral emotions, and moral behavior psychopathology and crime -- Deception: faking good or bad -- Aggression -- Personality disorder and crime -- Contemporary approaches to psychopathy -- Violent offenders: neurobiology and crime -- Safe community reintegration of sex offenders through circles of support and accountability -- Psychotic disorders and violence: what do we know so far -- Aggressive behavior in offenders with intellectual disabilities: theories and treatment -- Autism and (violent) offending: an overview of current knowledge, risk factors, and treatment risk assessment and rehabilitation -- Risk management in forensic psychiatry: integrating a social network approach -- Forensic rehabilitation: a phase of transition on a

	lifelong risk (and health) continuum.
Subjects	Forensic Psychiatry. Crime--psychology. Criminals--psychology. Dangerous Behavior. Mental Disorders--therapy. Mentally Ill Persons--legislation & jurisprudence.
Notes	Includes bibliographical references.

The mind of the criminal: the role of developmental social cognition in criminal defense law

LCCN	2011041597
Type of material	Book
Personal name	Fontaine, Reid Griffith, 1971-
Main title	The mind of the criminal: the role of developmental social cognition in criminal defense law / Reid Griffith Fontaine.
Published/Created	New York: Cambridge University Press, 2012.
Description	xv, 264 p.; 24 cm.
ISBN	9780521513760 (hardback) 0521513766 (hardback)
LC classification	KF9242 .F64 2012
Summary	"This book discusses the excusing nature of both traditional and nontraditional criminal law defenses and questions the structure of these defenses based on scientific findings from social and developmental psychology"-- Provided by publisher. "In American criminal law, if a defendant demonstrates that they lack certain psychological capabilities, they may be excused of blame and punishment for wrongdoing. However, criminal defense law often fails to consider the developmental science of individual differences in ability and functioning that may inform jurisprudential issues of rational capacity and responsibility in criminal law. This book discusses the excusing nature of a range of both traditional and nontraditional criminal law defenses and questions the structure of these defenses based on scientific findings from social and

	developmental psychology. This book explores how research on individual differences in the development of social perception, judgment, and decision making explain why some youths and adults develop psychological tendencies that favor criminal behavior, and considers how developmental science can guide the understanding of criminal excuses and affirmative defense law. "-- Provided by publisher.
Contents	Machine generated contents note: 1. A meeting of developmental social cognition and criminal jurisprudence and law; 2. Developmental social cognition and antisocial behavior: theory and science; 3. Substandard rational capacity and criminal responsibility; 4. Underdeveloped rationality and wrongdoing in youth; 5. Moral subrationality and the propensity for wrongdoing; 6. Provocation interpretational bias and heat of passion homicide; 7. Reacting to perceived threats: mistaken self-defense and duress; 8. Developmental social cognition, the effects of chronic abuse and trauma, and reactive homicide; 9. Toward a more psychologically-informed approach to social rationality and excusing conditions in criminal law.
Subjects	Defense (Criminal procedure)--United States. Insanity (Law)--United States. Criminal psychology--United States.
Notes	Includes bibliographical references and index.

The origins of American criminology

LCCN	2010026913
Type of material	Book
Main title	The origins of American criminology / Francis T. Cullen ... [et al.], editors.
Published/Created	New Brunswick, N.J.: Transaction Publishers, c2011.
Description	[vi], 433 p.; 24 cm.
ISBN	9781412814676 (alk. paper) 1412814677 (alk. paper)
LC classification	HV6022.U6 O75 2011
Related names	Cullen, Francis T.

Contents Clifford R. Shaw and Henry D. McKay: Chicago criminologists / Jon Snodgrass -- Edwin H. Sutherland: the development of differential association theory / Colin Goff and Gilbert Geis -- Communities and crime revisited: intellectual trajectory of a Chicago school education / Robert J. Sampson -- The making of criminology revisited: an oral history of Merton's anomie paradigm / Francis T. Cullen and Steven F. Messner -- The intellectual origins of institutional-anomie theory / Richard Rosenfeld and Steven F. Messner -- Revitalizing Merton: general strain theory / Robert Agnew -- Thorsten Sellin: culture conflict, crime, and beyond / Colin Goff and Gilbert Geis -- The Pennsylvania school of criminology: building tipping points for a discipline / Lawrence W. Sherman -- The rise of feminist criminology: Freda Adler / Jennifer L. Hartman and Jody L. Sundt -- Becoming a peacemaking criminologist: the travels of Richard Quinney / John F. Wozniak -- The origins of the routine activity approach and situational crime prevention / Ronald V. Clarke and Marcus Felson -- Because crime hurts, justice must heal: John Braithwaite / Nicole Leeper Piquero and Paul Mazerolle -- The origins and development of containment theory: Walt C. Reckless and Simon Dinitz / C. Ronald Huff and Frank R. Scarpitti -- Control theory: the life and work of Travis Hirschi / John H. Laub -- In pursuit of "A general theory of crime" / Michael R. Gottfredson -- The origins of me and of social learning theory: personal and professional recollections and reflections / Ronald L. Akers -- Sheldon and Eleanor Glueck's unraveling juvenile delinquency study: the lives of 1,000 Boston men in the twentieth century / John H. Laub and Robert J. Sampson -- Understanding the development of antisocial behavior: Terrie Moffitt / Alex R. Piquero.

Subjects Criminology--United States--History.

Notes Includes bibliographical references and index.

Series	Advances in criminological theory; v. 16 Advances in criminological theory; v. 16.

The origins of antisocial behavior: a developmental perspective

LCCN	2011048017
Type of material	Book
Main title	The origins of antisocial behavior: a developmental perspective / edited by Christopher R. Thomas and Kayla Pope.
Published/Created	Oxford; New York: Oxford University Press, c2013.
Description	xiii, 287 p.: ill.; 25 cm.
ISBN	9780199753475 (alk. paper)
LC classification	RC555 .O75 2013
Related names	Thomas, Christopher R. (Psychiatrist) Pope, Kayla.
Subjects	Antisocial personality disorders.
Notes	Includes bibliographical references and index.

The Routledge international handbook of biosocial criminology

LCCN	2014018248
Type of material	Book
Main title	The Routledge international handbook of biosocial criminology / edited by Matt DeLisi, Michael G Vaughn.
Edition	First Edition.
Published/Produced	London; New York: Routledge, Taylor & Francis Group, 2015.
Description	xxvii,660 pages; 26 cm.
Links	Cover image http://images.tandf.co.uk/common/jackets/websmall/978041572/9780415722131.jpg
ISBN	9780415722131 (hardback)
LC classification	HV6025 .R697 2015
Related names	DeLisi, Matt, editor of compilation. Vaughn, Michael G., editor of compilation.
Summary	"Biosocial criminology is an interdisciplinary field that aims to explain crime and antisocial behavior by exploring both biological factors and environmental factors. Since the mapping of the human genome,

scientists have been able to study the biosocial causes of human behaviour with the greatest specificity. After decades of almost exclusive sociological focus, criminology has undergone a paradigm shift where the field is more interdisciplinary and this book combines perspectives from criminology and sociology with contributions from fields such as genetics, neuropsychology, and evolutionary psychology. The Routledge International Handbook of Biosocial Criminology is the largest and most comprehensive work of its kind, and is organized into five sections that collectively span the terrain of biosocial research on antisocial behavior. Bringing together leading experts from around the world, this book considers the criminological, genetic and neuropsychological foundations of offending, as well as the legal and criminal justice applications of biosocial criminological theory and will be essential reading for students, researchers, and practitioners from across the social, behavioural, and natural sciences who are engaged in the study of antisocial behaviour. "--Provided by publisher.

"Biosocial criminology is an interdisciplinary field that aims to explain crime and antisocial behavior by exploring both biological factors and environmental factors. Since the mapping of the human genome, scientists have been able to study the biosocial causes of human behaviour with the greatest specificity. After decades of almost exclusive sociological focus, criminology has undergone a paradigm shift where the field is more interdisciplinary and this book combines perspectives from criminology and sociology with contributions from fields such as genetics, neuropsychology, and evolutionary psychology. The Routledge International Handbook of Biosocial Criminology is the largest and most comprehensive work of its kind, and is organized into five sections that collectively span the terrain of biosocial research on antisocial behavior. Bringing together leading

	experts from around the world, this book considers the criminological, genetic and neuropsychological foundations of offending, as well as the legal and criminal justice applications of biosocial criminological theory and will be essential reading for students, researchers, and practitioners from across the social, behavioural, and natural sciences who are engaged in the study of antisocial behaviour"-- Provided by publisher.
Subjects	Criminology. Criminal behavior--Psychological aspects. Criminal behavior--Genetic aspects. Human beings--Effect of environment on. Sociobiology. Psychology / Neuropsychology. Psychology / Social Psychology. Social Science / Criminology.
Series	Routledge international handbooks

The student's guide to social neuroscience

LCCN	2016020634
Type of material	Book
Personal name	Ward, Jamie, 1972- author.
Main title	The student's guide to social neuroscience / Jamie Ward.
Edition	2nd Edition.
Published/Produced	New York: Psychology Press, 2016.
ISBN	9781138908611 (hardback) 9781138908628 (pbk.)
LC classification	BF311 .W26947 2016
Contents	Introduction to social neuroscience -- The methods of social neuroscience -- Evolutionary origins -- Emotion and motivation -- Reading faces and bodies -- Understanding others -- Interacting with others -- Relationships -- Groups and identity -- Morality and antisocial behavior -- Developmental social neuroscience -- Example essay questions -- Recommended further reading -- .

Subjects	Perception. Social interaction.
Notes	Revised edition of the author's The student's guide to social neuroscience, 2012.
Additional formats	Online version: Ward, Jamie, 1972- author. Student's guide to social neuroscience 2nd Edition. New York: Psychology Press, 2016 9781315694306 (DLC) 2016021734

The veterans and active duty military psychotherapy progress notes planner

LCCN	2009031714
Type of material	Book
Personal name	Berghuis, David J.
Main title	The veterans and active duty military psychotherapy progress notes planner / by David J. Berghuis, Arthur E. Jongsma, Jr.
Published/Created	Hoboken, N.J.: John Wiley, c2010.
Description	xiv, 394 p.; 28 cm.
ISBN	9780470440971 (pbk.)
LC classification	UH629.3 .B47 2010
Related names	Jongsma, Arthur E., Jr., 1943-
Contents	Adjustment to killing -- Adjustment to the military culture -- Amputation, loss of mobility, disfigurement -- Anger management and domestic violence -- Antisocial behavior in the military -- Anxiety -- Attention and concentration deficits -- Bereavement due to the loss of a comrade -- Borderline personality -- Brief reactive psychotic episode -- Chronic pain after injury -- Combat and operational stress reaction -- Conflict with comrades -- Depression -- Diversity acceptance -- Financial difficulties -- Homesickness/loneliness -- Insomnia -- Traumatic brain injury -- Nightmares -- Opioid dependence -- Panic/agoraphobia -- Parenting problems related to deployment -- Performance-enhancing supplement use -- Phobia -- Physiological stress response -- Post-deployment reintegration problems -- Posttraumatic stress disorder (PTSD) -- Pre-deployment stress --

	Separation and divorce -- Sexual assault by another service member -- Shift work sleep disorder -- Social discomfort -- Spiritual and religious issues -- Substance abuse/dependence -- Suicidal ideation -- Survivor's guilt -- Tobacco use.
Subjects	Veterans--Mental health--United States--Handbooks, manuals, etc. Soldiers--Mental health--United States--Handbooks, manuals, etc. Psychotherapy--Planning--Handbooks, manuals, etc. Psychology, Military--Handbooks, manuals, etc.
Notes	Includes bibliographical references.
Series	PracticePlanners series

Violent offenders: understanding and assessment

LCCN	2014022204
Type of material	Book
Main title	Violent offenders: understanding and assessment / edited by Christina A. Pietz, Curtis A. Mattson.
Published/Produced	New York: Oxford University Press, 2015.
Description	xi, 549 pages; 24 cm
ISBN	9780199917297 (pbk.: alk. paper)
LC classification	RC569.5.V55 V59 2015
Related names	Pietz, Christina A., editor. Mattson, Curtis A.
Contents	About the editors -- Contributors -- Overview and constructs of violence -- Psychological perspectives of violence / Melanie Schettler -- Antisocial behavior among children in poverty: understanding environmental effects in daily life / Michael A. Russell and Candice L. Odgers -- Substance abuse and violence / Curtis A. Mattson and Christina A. Pietz -- Major mental disorders and violence / Laura S. Guy and Kevin S. Douglas -- Aggressive externalizing disorders: conduct disorder, antisocial personality disorder, and psychopathy / Laura E. Drislane, Noah C. Venables, and Christopher J. Patrick -- Special offender populations -- Juvenile homicide: trends, correlates, causal factors, and outcomes / Kathleen M.

Heide -- Physically and sexually violent females / Geoffrey R. McKee and R. Gregg Dwyer -- Homicide: a national and global perspective / Bethany K. Walters and Eric W. Hickey -- Psychological factors in intimate partner violence / Donald Dutton and Christie Tetreault -- Perpetrators of sexual violence: demographics, assessments, interventions / Alix M. McLearen, Ivonne E. Bazerman, and Katherine Bracken-Minor -- Under the color of authority: police officers as violent offenders / David M. Corey and Casey O. Stewart -- Institutional violence risk: theory, assessment, and management / Daniel J. Neller and Michael J. Vitacco -- Youth gangs: an overview of key findings and directions for the future / Terrance J. Taylor and J. Michael Vecchio -- Understanding terrorists / Randy Borum -- Evaluative approach and special considerations -- Legal, clinical and scientific foundations of violence risk assessment / David F. Mrad and Daniel J. Neller -- Use of assessment measures for the evaluation of future risk / Chad A. Brinkley -- The structured professional judgment approach to violence risk assessment and management: why it is useful, how to use it, and its empirical support / Kevin S. Douglas and Henrik Belfrage -- Assessing facets of personality and psychopathology in violent offenders / Dustin B. Wygant, Kathryn C. Applegate, and Tina D. Wall -- Assessing malingering in violent offenders / Holly A. Miller -- Assessment of neurophysiological and neuropsychological bases for violence / Rachel Fazio and Robert L. Denney -- Violence: psychiatric assessment and intervention / Charles Scott, Philip J. Resnick, and William Newman -- Ethical considerations and professional roles in working with violent offenders / Kimberly Larson, Robert Kinscherff, and Stacey Goldstein -- Conducting research with special populations / Gianni Pirelli and Patricia A. Zapf -- Index.

Subjects Violent offenders--Psychology.

Notes Includes index.

RELATED NOVA PUBLICATIONS

ANTISOCIAL BEHAVIOR: ETIOLOGY, GENETIC AND ENVIRONMENTAL INFLUENCES AND CLINICAL MANAGEMENT

Editor: Justine H. Gallo

ISBN: 978-1-63321-521-4 Publication Date: 2014

Parents play a central role in the lives of their children. Parent-child interaction is a central variable in the etiology of antisocial behaviour. Research suggests that families of antisocial individuals are characterized by harsh and inconsistent discipline, little positive parental involvement and poor monitoring and supervision. Thus parents could create environments for unhealthy parent-child relationships with subsequent antisocial behaviour of their adolescents. This book discusses several topics that may lead to antisocial behavior. It describes the etiology, genetic and environmental influences, as well as clinical management of antisocial behavior.

LIFE COURSE PERSISTENT ANTISOCIAL BEHAVIOR: A REVIEW*

Robert Eme, Ph.D.
Illinois School of Professional Psychology at Argosy University, Schaumburg Campus, Schaumburg, IL, US

A half a century ago Lee Robins landmark research, which found that severe adult antisocial behavior virtually requires childhood antisocial behavior, helped launch the study of the developmental origins of antisocial behavior and provided the initial empirical basis for the classic formulation of the developmental category of Life Course Persistent Antisocial Behavior. The importance of this category for the study of crime and criminal behavior can scarcely be exaggerated given the robust and remarkable finding that a small group of individuals (5-10%), almost all male, who tend to cluster in this category are responsible for over half of all crimes in the United States and other developed countries, and an even greater proportion of violent crimes. This chapter reviewed the status of this category and as well as its importance for providing future directions for the study of crime and criminal behavior in the next half century.

* The full version of this chapter can be found in *Crime and Criminal Behavior*, edited by Analise Klein, published by Nova Science Publishers, Inc, New York, 2016.

SPANISH PARENTING STYLES AND ANTISOCIAL BEHAVIOR IN ADOLESCENTS[*]

Maite Garaigordobil[*], *Vanesa Martínez and Aida Fernández*
Department of Personality, Evaluation and Psychological Treatment, Faculty of Psychology, University of the Basque Country, Donostia-San Sebastián, Spain

The purpose of the study was to explore the connections of antisocial behavior with the degree of parents' acceptance-involvement and coercion-imposition, as well as the different parenting styles (authoritative, authoritarian, neglectful, and indulgent). The sample comprised 3,026 participants from the Basque Country (Spain), aged between 12 and 18 years (48.5% males, 51.5% females). Three assessment instruments were administered: Antisocial-Delinquent Behaviors Questionnaire (Seisdedos, 1988/1995), Behavioral Problems Scale (Navarro et al., 1993) and Parental Socialization Scale for Adolescence (Musitu & García, 2001). The results confirm that a high level of acceptance-involvement and a low level of coercion-imposition of both parents are significantly associated with a low level of adolescents' antisocial behavior. The parents' degree of acceptance-involvement was an educational variable with considerable influence on the inhibition of the adolescents' antisocial behavior, and it had a greater weight than the degree of coercion-imposition used by the parents. The indulgent style (high acceptance-involvement and low coercion-imposition) was the most positive because participants who had indulgent parents displayed significantly lower levels of antisocial behavior. The authoritarian parenting style (low acceptance-involvement and high coercion-imposition) was the one that promoted the most antisocial behavior in the adolescents. The authoritarian and neglectful styles were the most harmful regarding antisocial behavior.

[*] The full version of this chapter can be found in *Parenting: Cultural Influences and Impact on Childhood Health and Well-Being*, edited by Fernando Garcia, published by Nova Science Publishers, Inc, New York, 2015.

[*] Corresponding Author: Maite Garaigordobil, Department of Personality, Evaluation and Psychological Treatment, Faculty of Psychology, University of the Basque Country, Avda. de Tolosa 70, 20018 Donostia-San Sebastián, Spain, Phone: 34-943-015634, Fax: 34-943-015670, http://www.sc.ehu.es/garaigordobil Email: maite.garaigordobil@ehu.es

Participants with authoritative parents (high acceptance-involvement and high coercion-imposition) showed lower levels of antisocial behavior than those with authoritarian parents, but no significant differences were found with the neglectful style. The results suggest the importance of programs targeting the parents to foster positive parental attitudes that inhibit antisocial behavior.

Exposure to Antisocial and Risk Behavior Media Content Stimulates Cyberbullying Behavior: The Cyclic Process Model*

Anouk den Hamer† *and Elly Konijn*
VU University Amsterdam,
Dept. of Communication Science, Section Media Psychology

Ten years ago, cyberbullying behavior, or bullying carried out via electronic media, was a relatively new phenomenon (Smith, 2014). Over the last ten years, research investigating cyberbullying has accumulated rapidly. At first, the majority of research was descriptive in nature and scholars tried to determine how many children and adolescents were victims of cyberbullying or cyberbullies themselves. Results showed that cyberbullying peaks during adolescence and between 10% to 40% of adolescents have been a victim of cyberbullying (Kowalski, Giumetti, Schroeder, and Lattanner, 2014; Tokunaga, 2010). Much research has focused on the negative impact of cyberbullying and how victims cope with it. For example, being victimized through cyberbullying relates to a number of psychosocial difficulties, such as depression, anxiety, and stress (e.g., Campbell, Spears, Slee, Butler, and Kift, 2012; Gamez-Guadix, Orue, Smith, and Calvete, 2013; Gradinger, Strohmeier, and Spiel, 2009; Wang, Nansel, and Iannotti, 2011), suicidal ideation (e.g., Bauman, Toomey, and Walker, 2013; Hay and Meldrum, 2010; Hinduja and Patchin, 2010; Sinclair, Bauman, Poteat, Koenig, and Russel, 2012), and poorer academic achievement (e.g., Kowalski and Limber, 2013; Sinclair et al., 2012). Furthermore, numerous studies have showed that having been

* The full version of this chapter can be found in *A Social-Ecological Approach to Cyberbullying*, edited by Michelle F. Wright, published by Nova Science Publishers, Inc, New York, 2015.

† Corresponding Author Email: a.h.den.hamer@vu.nl.

victimized by offline or online bullying is related to being or becoming a cyberbullying perpetrator (Bauman, 2010; König, Gollwitzer, and Steffgen, 2010; Kowalski, Morgan, and Limber, 2012; Patchin and Hinduja, 2011; Smith, Mahdavi, Carvalho, Fisher, Russel, and Tippett, 2008; Sontag, Clemans, Graber, and Lyndon, 2011; Wong, Chan, Cheng, 2014; Wright and Li, 2012; Wright and Li, 2013; Ybarra and Mitchell, 2004; Yilmaz, 2011). The relationship between being victimized (i.e., being bullied) and becoming a cyberbully is striking because one might expect that these victims understand the impact of being bullied and would not harm others in such an unpleasant situation. Therefore, we investigated the underlying processes that take place in the relationship between victimization and cyberbullying behavior.

In the current chapter, we provide arguments for a Cyclic Process Model as a framework to investigate the relation between being bullied and becoming a cyberbully. To clarify this relationship, the Cyclic Process Model proposes that victimized adolescents get angry and frustrated, which draws them to media with antisocial and risk behavior content, further easing the way to become a cyberbully. Thus far, the role of adolescent media use in this chain of events has been understudied. Therefore, our research focused on the role of media use in cyberbullying behavior. In the following section, we first provide a short overview of the current state of cyberbullying research. Next, the role of media in cyberbullying behavior is discussed and the Cyclic Process Model is introduced. In addition, we provide empirical tests of the Cyclic Process Model with different samples showing the underlying, amplifying role of media use. The chapter concludes with a summary of the findings, limitations, and challenges in view of future research.

A Nonhuman Primate Model of Serotonin-Mediated Violence and Antisocial Behavior—A Decade-and-a-Half Update*

Whitney F. Espinel and J. Dee Higley†
Department of Psychology, Brigham Young University,
Provo, UT, US

This chapter reviews and updates the state of the nonprimate model of serotonin-mediated antisocial behavior, impulsivity, and violent aggression. Evidence is presented showing that as with the behavioral and temperamental traits that are mediated by serotonin, interindividual differences in central serotonin functioning (as measured by CSF 5-HIAA concentrations) is trait-like, showing stability across time and situation. Data are reviewed showing male and female macaques with low CNS serotonin functioning are impulsive and violent. They exhibit impulsive behaviors, such as spontaneous long dangerous leaps between treetops, are trapped more often, and exhibit risky behaviors when there is an opportunity for reward. They are also more likely to perpetrate severe, violent aggression. High rates of impulsivity are positively correlated with violent or escalated aggression. Perhaps as a result of these behaviors, subjects with low CSF 5-HIAA concentrations are often wounded and die prematurely from violent means, particularly males. Socially, they are often loners, less competent in social interactions, and antisocial in their natures. While males and females with low CSF 5-HIAA concentrations show similar impulsivity, studies are reviewed showing sex differences in how these serotonin-mediated traits are manifest, as well as sex differences in the targets of violence and aggression. Although most of these studies are correlational in design, there is evidence of a causal effect. Pharmacological agents or diet changes that augment central serotonin decrease rates of aggression while conversely agents that diminish central serotonin increase aggression. Recent studies investigating genetic effects have assessed the serotonin transporter gene (rh5-HTT) and its relationship to transporter

* The full version of this chapter can be found in *Serotonin: Biosynthesis, Regulation and Health Implications*, edited by Frank Scott Hall, published by Nova Science Publishers, Inc, New York, 2013.

† Corresponding Author Email: James_Higley@byu.edu.

binding in the brain as well as levels of CSF 5-HIAA concentrations. These studies suggest the serotonin transporter genotype may be related to differences in aggression and impulsivity and other negative emotions. Specifically, macaques with one or two copies of the rh5-HTT short allele may exhibit aggressive tendencies, more impulsive errors, and social alienation while carriers of two long alleles tend to be more placid and gregarious in temperament. Substantial evidence shows that the phenotypic expression of the genotypes are mediated by the environment, with early rearing, sex, situational variables, and the genotype of a partner affecting the phenotypic expression of the rh5-HTT gene.

Antisocial Behavior in Children with ADHD: Causes and Treatment[*]

Efrosini Kalyva

Senior Lecturer, City College, Thessaloniki, Greece

Attention Deficit/Hyperactivity Disorder (ADHD) is a prevalent disorder among school aged children and adolescents worldwide. Many children and adolescents with ADHD exhibit antisocial behavior that usually takes the form of aggression or conduct disorder. This chapter starts with definitions of ADHD and antisocial behaviors, while it reviews recent studies on the aetiology of this behavior. Since genes and physiology alone do not determine behavior, emphasis will be placed also on the role that the environment plays in creating and shaping certain antisocial behaviors. There will be reference to academic and social underachievement that may trigger antisocial behavior in children and young adults with ADHD, as well as other family factors. The last part of the chapter will focus on interventions that can effectively address the antisocial behavior of children and adolescents with ADHD and involve not only individuals, but also their families and their communities.

---

[*] The full version of this chapter can be found in *Social Psychology: New Developments*, edited by Jan M. Turner and Andrew D. Mitchell, published by Nova Science Publishers, Inc, New York, 2012.

INTERNET ADDICTION AND ANTISOCIAL INTERNET BEHAVIOR OF ADOLESCENTS*

Hing Keung Ma†
Department of Education Studies, Hong Kong Baptist University, Hong Kong, PRC

Internet addiction and the moral implication of antisocial Internet behavior will be investigated in this paper. More and more people use the Internet in their daily life. Unfortunately the percentage of people who use the internet excessively also increases. The concept of Internet addiction or pathological use of Internet is discussed in detail, and the characteristics of Internet addicts are also delineated. The social, (especially the antisocial), use of Internet is discussed. It is argued that the behavior of Internet use is similar to daily life social behavior. In other words, Internet behavior is a kind of social behavior. Kohlberg's theory of moral development is employed to delineate the moral reasoning of the antisocial Internet behavior. The following behaviors are regarded as antisocial Internet behavior: 1) the use of Internet to carry out illegal activities such as selling faked products or offensive pornographic materials, 2) the use of Internet to bully others (i.e., cyberbullying) such as distributing libelous statements against a certain person, 3) the use of Internet to cheat others and 4) to use Internet to do illegal gambling. The characteristics of the moral stages that are associated with these antisocial Internet behaviors are investigated in detail.

* The full version of this chapter can be found in *Positive Youth Development: A New School Curriculum to Tackle Adolescent Developmental Issues*, edited by Hing Keung Ma, Daniel TL Shek and Joav Merrick, published by Nova Science Publishers, Inc, New York, 2012.

† Corresponding Author: Professor Hing Keung Ma, BSc, DipEd, PhD, Faculty of Social Sciences, Department of Education Studies (RL2-1/F), Hong Kong Baptist University, University Road Campus, Kowloon Tong, Hong Kong, PRC. E-mail: hkma@hkbu.edu.hk.

INDEX

D

E

F

G

H

I

J

K

L

M

Q

R

S

T

U

V

W

X

Y